Praise for *Drug Mu*

CW00925149

"Top journalist Joanne Joseph has tak[...] [...] drug trafficking and given it new perspective and new life. The tragic story of beauty Vanessa Goosen, jailed for drug trafficking in Thailand while pregnant, becomes not just a Papillon-like epic of triumph of the human spirit over adversity, but reads like a top-drawer thriller too. I was gripped from the first line." – **Justice Malala, columnist and talk show host**

"The quality of the writing is such that you are actually there. You are at the airport, the court and the jail. You suffer the unbearable lows and surprising highs of the experience and will cry when you finally get your freedom. You will experience and you will think. This book should be compulsory reading for school kids and all who are easily led into temptation. I read it in one sitting." – **John Robbie, Talk Radio 702**

"*Drug Muled* is a view from the mule's side. Fast paced and written in the first person, it is Vanessa's view and conversation with herself and us about her predicament and the pitfalls of love. Joanne captures the tension, confusion, anger and desolation of Vanessa and takes the reader into the putrid smells and battles with mosquitoes and rats that make up Thailand's Lard Yao prison jungle. Intoxicating may be the wrong pun, but the book comes close." – **Mathatha Tsedu, journalist and commentator**

"… a riveting, compelling and powerfully written narrative." – **Jeremy Maggs, broadcaster**

"Right from the opening line this gripping story, as told by distinguished broadcaster Joanne Joseph, makes for compelling reading. It is more than just an account of a bad turn of fate in the life of a beauty queen – it is a thriller, excellently written, cautioning the gullible against falling prey to unscrupulous drug smugglers." – **Riaan Cruywagen, veteran broadcaster**

"I am so proud of Vanessa for sharing her experiences in this book for all the world to see. Her life is a stunning example of someone who is willing to make a difference and prevent a repeat of what she went through." – **Dr Marlin McKay, 3Talk medical expert**

"With gripping detail, Joanne Joseph tells the moving story of Vanessa Goosen's horrific experience tangled up in the Thai justice system. This is a story about a woman's monumental strength, her will to survive and her deep love for her daughter. It is a story that reminds us of the resilience of the human spirit; a story that will leave every reader inspired." – **AE Ballakisten, poet**

"The authenticity of this gripping human drama is successfully preserved by author Joanne Joseph's decision to tell the story of convicted drug mule, Vanessa Goosen, in the former Miss South Africa finalist's own words. Joseph captures the Thai jail hell Goosen endured for 16 years without ever judging her subject's choices. When you put this book down you may also find it difficult to judge. A compelling read." – **Nkepile Mabuse, CNN correspondent**

"*Drug Muled* opens up a hidden world into drug trafficking, and forces us to ask 'what if it was me?'. It asks us to question our assumptions about what this dark corner of global trade actually entails." – **Karabo Kgoleng, arts journalist**

Drug Muled

Drug Muled
Sixteen Years in a Thai Prison
The Vanessa Goosen Story

By Joanne Joseph

with Larissa Focke

MF BOOKS JOBURG

First published by MFBooks Joburg,
an imprint of Jacana Media (Pty) Ltd, in 2013

10 Orange Street
Sunnyside
Auckland Park 2092
South Africa
+2711 628 3200
www.jacana.co.za

ISBN 978-1-920601-20-1

Cover design by publicide
Set in Sabon 11/15pt
Printed and bound by Ultra Litho (Pty) Ltd, Johannesburg
Job no. 001966

See a complete list of Jacana titles at www.jacana.co.za

"I realise what they did to us in there – what they did to me. How they turned me into a savage, only half human, bathing in a trough and eating food fit for animals, and locking me in a cage every night."
– Vanessa Goosen, 2013

Contents

CHAPTER 1

Open your bag

"Open your bag, please ma'am..." he smiles.

Inoffensive but insistent. The white crispness of his Colgate smile broken only by the glitter of gold teeth. He's the Man in Green and Black. Polite and portly. Glued to the airport scanner like it's broadcasting a soccer match. She's watched him since she joined the queue. He jokes with every passenger, laughs out loud. Disarms them while he carries out his detailed surveillance. He studies every feature in every passport, every line in every face, like a portrait he'll soon commit to his sketchpad. Then he's chatty again, telling more jokes. A comedian in uniform. Poster-boy for this Land of a Thousand Smiles, deferring to his trusty scanner – the mechanised oracle that reveals all.

But she's not in the mood for this childishness. She wants this over with. She can't turn her back on Bangkok fast enough. It blisters, bristles, boils. A steaming cauldron of souls thronging streets, clogging alleyways, choking market places. Far away from the sultriness of sand-meets-sea at the luxury resorts, the grit of Thailand, of everyday, pithy Thailand, bears down on her, has made her irritable and breathless – even as she rushed toward the airport to board a plane home, injecting herself into this long, snaking line.

For six days she's been swept up in this – in the smells that

1

sting her nostrils, the heat that smoulders feverishly under her skin and melts the pavements under her feet. She's been carried by the current of clammy bodies, unseen, down Bangkok's main roads, into its exotic markets, through the estuaries of side streets where the hiss of street cooking fills the air and sexworkers stand plugged into their cigarettes, inhaling deeply.

She's still bewildered at how the colours, the sounds rushed at her, stampeded over her in those streets. Thousands of people transacting, trading right there on the sidewalks, as though the shops had all exhaled their wares onto the cluttered pavements. It's all for sale. Food. Fashion. Fornication. The world of the flesh sitting slap-bang in the middle of a weird reverence. The swinging Buddha dangling hypnotically from the taxi driver's mirror. The shrines on almost every street where locals stand reverently, their heads bowed, their palms pressed together. The simplest gifts of flowers, fruit or glowing incense sticks send their prayers wafting, a slither of smoke soon forgotten, before the worshipper disappears hopefully into the throng.

No, she can't romanticise this city – not like the other tourists hanging like unruly branches from the backs of motorbikes or weaving through the muddled, mis-stitched tapestry of its streets in tuk tuks, drinking up every detail their eyes fall on. Most of all, the heat weighs on her like a sweaty lover with his slow, heavy overtures and rancid breath. And almost every meal she's eaten since arriving has seen her, knees hammered to the floor, head clamped over toilet bowl, retching till she's spent.

None of it sits well with her – not the reality of being alone and foreign in this place that feels a world away from her own, or the strangeness of people who've crossed her path in the last few days with their threatening presence and bizarre requests. She's upset with herself for being too naïve. She was in too much of a hurry to set off on this trip without enough forethought or adequate planning. And from the moment she's joined this check-in queue, she's become impatient and prickly. Her legs stiltish, unsteady, weakened by the emptiness of a clawing stomach. She'd put her hand to it. To protect it from the other passengers' bodies crushed *too close. A reminder she was not entirely alone.*

The scent of a hundred bodies has risen up in her nostrils, while the Man in Green and Black spreads his silly humour and oversees bags being flung open and the minutiae of peoples' lives exposed – the colour of their undies, the cheap gifts destined for chubby hands, their penchant for porn. And she's mentally pushed her way to the front of this queue. It's been all that's kept her from crashing to the floor with exhaustion – the thought of lunging through that metal portal, bag skidding in her wake, racing across the tarmac to the waiting plane with its low hum, its engines firing, its promise of home as it kicks away the ground beneath. Daring to think of the man who'll wrap himself around her and take her to his bed where she'll dream warmly.

"Ma'am – please, open your bag!"

She's suddenly wrenched back here, to the front of this queue. She shouldn't have kept him waiting. He asks so nicely. She finds herself nodding in agreement, distracted, a passive spectator, while he gestures that he's happy to do it himself. He is rifling through, whistling a tune to himself – the theme song from some cartoon. He scratches at the magazines, stacking them aside to paw at something underneath. It's the books. "Hey! Be careful with those... they're not mine!" she says in passing.

She wishes he would hurry up. A quiet desperation comes over her. She has to leave this sweltering place right now to get to her life on the other side. But he has no idea – this man standing there with his toothy smile, broken English and small knife that appears out of nowhere. And it's the last thing she expects from him, but suddenly, in her mind, his smile has turned mocking, sadistic even. And like a butcher, he is raising the glinting blade, brandishing it – thrusting it into the spine, slashing, ripping, disembowelling the book! "NO!" she is shouting. "What are you...?!"

But his eyes have lit up, as though he's hit the jackpot.

"What is this?" he says, teasingly.

And she looks down. And she suddenly understands...

And though her funnyman is still grinning, it chills her from skin to sinew to bone. Because amid the fury of this wet heat and

the sweat that drips from her, it is falling.
Falling like off-white snow.
Like a pile of pristine fluffy innocence.
He points to a poster on the wall.
"Heroin is death sentence," he laughs.
This time, she knows he's not joking.

CHAPTER 2

Interrogation

"One minute please. You come with me!"

He leads me down a series of corridors lit by a stab of artificial light. His steps are powerful but heavy, his short legs dragging his stocky body along. I trot alongside him like a frightened animal, terrified of this place he's taking me to. A ring of sweat gathers where he puts his hand in the small of my back. My heart punches my ribs. My mind barrels. *What the hell was in the books? Cocaine? How the hell did it get there?! Planted?! Jackson's brother, Obey?*

My mind tears backwards to the night the phone in my hotel room rings. It's late. It must be Felix! I lunge for it. I'm dying to hear his voice. But instead...

"Hey Vanessa – Jackson here! I got your number from Felix. Listen man, I was wondering if you could buy some Police-branded clothing for me. I'll pay you back as soon as you get back home."

I'm bitterly disappointed. "Oh, yes, hi Jackson. Sure. Tell me exactly what you want."

He rattles off a list which I scribble down. And as I'm about to hang up – "Hey Vanessa, do you think you can bring back some engineering books for me? My brother's in Bangkok. He can bring them to your hotel."

How can I say no? He's Felix's friend. We make small talk about the terrible food and how I was mugged on the street the

5

other day. He has lots of advice for me.

"Check out a place called the Woodland Inn. It's much cheaper. And you might like the food better."

And just a few days later, that's exactly where Jackson's brother, Obey, finds me. He's smartly dressed in a well-put-together outfit, the look broken only by the cap on top of his large head. Fish eyed and dark skinned, he smells of confidence. A plastic bag hangs at his side.

"Wow! Jackson didn't tell me you were so beautiful."

A weird thing to say to a complete stranger. But as he stands there, his tongue hanging out like a thirsty dog, I wish I'd changed out of this figure-hugging skirt that exposes my belly button, before answering the door. He stands there mesmerised, as though he's never laid eyes on female flesh before. I want to wriggle out of his stare. He pulls some food out of the bag. "This is for you. Jackson told me you don't like the food here."

He sits at the edge of the bed. "You know, you shouldn't get involved with guys from here," he says.

"That's not what I'm here for," I say. "I have a boyfriend, *and* I'm pregnant." He's shocked. "No way!" he says. "You're so small and your stomach is so flat."

Inside my head I can feel my mind churning, trying to figure out a way to get rid of him. He's creepy and I don't like him. He reaches over and caresses my hand. I shove his away.

"I don't appreciate you touching me." I say firmly. "Are these the books you want me to take to your brother?" They're thick, A4 hardcover textbooks full of complicated technical drawings. Obey tries his luck one last time. He wants to take me out. "No thanks. I'm quite tired. I'd like to have a nap." He lumbers towards me to stifle me in a rugby tackle hug. But I side-step him and show him the door. I never see him again.

Now I keep asking myself, is he the reason I'm standing here, shaking with fear in this interrogation room? Everything is wildly chaotic in here. It's loud. There are so many people thrashing in and out of here. Some are yelling, others are laughing boisterously as they move around in this crush of people. And I'm sitting there, dead quiet. Frightened and confused because no one wants to talk to me, to tell me what's going on, even though I'm pleading with them.

There are three benches and a wooden table inside. I sit on one of these benches while the Man in Green and Black hauls out my bags and spreads them on the table before me. He and his friends chuckle and speak at the top of their voices while they pull out the books one by one. They savagely strip them of their front and back covers. And I watch the powder waterfall flow again. This time it seems endless. Every granule is emptied into a bowl on a scale that groans under its weight. There are four hidden compartments on the front and back of each book. Books that looked so ordinary to me. But the pouring continues, a funnelling of fine dust that clouds the air above it. The heap swells until it looks like a small mountain. Once all the packaging's removed, there are 1.7 kilograms of drugs in all.

They're searching for more now. Pulling out their pointed rods, pushing, prodding the other items in my bag. Searching the bottom of my luggage for hidden compartments. Ripping through the seams of some of the clothing to see if anything's hidden there. They seem so excited by what they've found in the books, they start to shout at me like I'm deaf, *"Who give you this? Where you get this from?"*

And though my mouth is pasty and dry and my voice is crackly, I shout back, "They're not my books!"

"Where you from?"

"South Africa," I say. "...And if you just phone Jackson, or my boyfriend Felix, they'll tell you that these books don't belong to me... I don't even know Obey..."

The Man in Green and Black has never stopped smiling, although it looks more like a smirk now. He grabs me and moves me over to a world map hanging on the wall. "Point. Where you come from?" And my finger goes straight to South Africa. "No, no, no! No Africa!" he begins shaking his head. "You not black. You from Pakistan. Fake passport. And your boyfriend, Nigerian."

"I am! I am South African! And these books are not mine! They belong to Obey. I don't know anything about the powder! Phone Jackson, phone Felix! They will tell you."

What's wrong with these people? Why won't they listen to what I say?

"You know what is this?" the Man in Green and Black asks.

"No."

"Look here!" He pulls out a small test tube that contains water. He takes a pinch of the powder, tosses it into the tube and shakes it hard. I watch it turn purplish blue. "This heroin!" he cries, amused. He's laughing. I am gasping. "Heroin? I've never even heard of heroin before…!" How do I convince this man I'm innocent? I know nothing about what's in these bags. How do I reason with him when he won't listen to a word I say?

And while the others snigger, another man comes up to me and presses his hand to my forehead. It's cold and damp like the limb of a corpse. "No worry. You only stay inside ten year," he laughs and those around him join in. I'm so humiliated – I hate them! And as this thought enters my mind, the Man in Green and Black and a female officer herd me towards the other side of the room. There's a curtain hanging there with a bed behind it. They tell me to lie down. I do as I'm told. But then I look at their machines and it hits me that they're about to X-ray me. At the time, I don't know they're looking for drugs in my system. I jump up and try to explain that I can't be X-rayed because I'm pregnant. There's a chair next to the pole. I fling myself onto the chair and grab the pole. "No, no! No X-ray!" I say. "Baby." I point to my stomach and mimic carrying an infant in my arms.

They're suspicious. They don't believe me. The woman tries to prise my fingers from the pole. But I've found a blast of raw strength that keeps my fingers glued there. And when they see how stubborn I am, they finally give up.

I get up to make my way back to the bench when I feel my stomach churning – the acid rising from deep within and launching up my throat. I clamp a hand to my mouth, trying to hold back the vomit. I see the bathroom door and run towards it. I make it in the nick of time, the liquid gushing out of me. But the female officer is behind me and she won't let me shut the door. *Let me vomit in peace!* But she's already shoving my head away, looking into the toilet bowl in case I've just expelled any more drugs from my system.

And the whole time, there's a torrent of officials entering the interrogation room. I take my chances, crying, appealing to every single one who walks in to help me, to phone Felix. Please! They laugh in my face and break into rapid Thai so that I can't understand a word spewing from their mouths. My cramping stomach won't hold a thing anymore. I'm rushing to the toilet every few minutes with diarrhoea, the Thai guard on my heels. The blistering heat saps me, making every step a huge effort.

And that's how time warps from seconds into minutes into hours. Three hours. Four hours flash by in a blur. The loud chatter and deafening laughter like a gong in my ears. A horde of journalists and cameramen suddenly burst in. They dazzle me with the flash of their bulbs. It's blinding. I hide my face under my coat. My picture will travel across oceans – the drug-peddling model, now too afraid to show her face. But there, in that small pocket of darkness, is partial silence. And I suddenly realise that while I've been sitting here for hours spilling my guts and screaming my innocence, my plane has left. All those travellers lining up ahead of me and behind me are now tucked away safely above me in the sky. How could they have left without me – the one person who longed to be on that flight bound for home? I raise my head. I look at the heroin death poster once more. It terrifies me. My plane is gone. My rights are gone. My freedom is gone. And the next thing I may lose is my life.

CHAPTER 3

Holding cells

The next seven days will teach me one of the hardest lessons of my life. Despite all those around you, the busyness and the noise of it all, in the end, you're completely alone in the world. The loneliness creeps in like a parasite in the dark, hooks itself in your gut and sucks at your insides. And there's a trail of emptiness it leaves as it slithers along.

For a few moments at Don Muang Airport that April afternoon, I'm the infamous Vanessa Leone Goosen. Beauty-queen-turned-businesswoman-turned-drug-mule. I give these airport police a few moments of high drama. Turn them into heroes in this battle the Thai people are losing against drugs. They'll tell their families stories about me tonight. How they caught a foreigner who carries her filth across borders. The filth that's heated and burnt and sniffed and injected and ruins lives. In this Thai war on drugs, if they find it on you, it's yours. No one cares where it came from. The chain of those involved in bringing it to this point is of no interest. As long as someone pays for every Thai child lying dead in a ditch somewhere with his veins black and blue. A life for a life.

And that's why mine has no value here. Once the press has seen my misery, burnt it into celluloid, they abruptly leave. So do my captors, as though there's nothing more to keep them interested. Now, only one remains – an officer who sits there in plain clothes on the bench next to me, casually reading a newspaper while my life disintegrates around me. And suddenly, I irrationally hope this man is my last chance. I feel the urge to try one last time to get him to listen to me.

With my freedom, my future, slipping away from me, I need to grab something, clutch at something concrete, that will end this nightmare. I have to fight. I know that. But after the callousness of these people, their insensitivity, their blindness to the truth, I really need just one shred of humanity. Just a one-minute gesture – a hand on my shoulder, a whispered reassurance to break through my fear that there's no way out of this; that trapped here, in the bowels of this airport, no one will forget me until my body turns up in a morgue somewhere.

I lunge forward and grab the officer's arm. "Help me! *Please help me!*" The tears burst from my eyes. My screaming gets louder. "I beg you. Those are not my drugs! Help me, I'm begging you!" My grip tightens. I drive my nails into him. "*Mai-daai*! *Maidaai!*" (No! No!) he shouts in Thai, grabbing at my fingers, forcing them from his arm. "Help me!" I won't let go – I can't. But he breaks free and spins backwards in shock as if I've tried to attack him, his eyes bulging at the madness of my actions. I don't care what he thinks of me – what any of them thinks of me. I lose my grip on the wooden bench and collapse onto the floor, screaming, begging, sobbing, pleading, squeezing my words out through the tightness of my throat, guttural and garbled. He grabs my arm and cuffs me to the bench.

"Oh God, Oh God, Oh God!" I cry. I feel myself choking between every sob. "Felix, help me! Help me, Felix! *Where the fuck are you?*"

The walls can't be that thick because one man hears me and comes in. He has terrible skin. Rocky moonface skin, full of craters. He sees me lying on the floor, bawling, yelling, lashing out, praying. And when he touches my shoulder, he makes me feel human again. I pick up my head to look at him. I can only imagine what he sees in my face. Black streams of mascara streaking my cheeks. The snaking veins of my red eyes. The madness of my dishevelled hair.

I clear my throat. "Please help me," I beg. "They're not my books. I swear to you – I'm not lying. Call Felix... please..." He looks at me for a moment – do I see a flash of sympathy there?

"I help you, but calm down. You hurt your baby."

It almost blinds me. The first real chink of hope I've glimpsed in the blackness of this day. He believes me when I've said I'm pregnant. He's a Drug Enforcement Administration agent who speaks relatively good English and understands me. He's willing to take my statement. In that moment he's everything to me: my saviour, my lifeline. His presence lifts my spirits and hope gushes in.

"Write down the telephone numbers, and I make sure someone calls Jackson or Felix," the officer assures me. "Don't worry. I try my best to help you." Once my statement's been taken, two thick Thai guards are called into the room. The air rushes in. It smells so different to the stuffiness of this room that reeks of human waste now. The officer tells me I'll be taken to a police station. The guards handcuff me. I watch them latch the cuffs, hear them click. They look like someone else's hands. I've crossed the line from law-abiding citizen to criminal.

As the men sandwich me between them, a flimsy filling, the officer who has become an angel comes over to me and gingerly wraps an old jersey around my wrists. It hides the gleaming metal of the handcuffs. And I hope it'll hide my shame. But still, every pair of eyes outside bores into me, all those people shaking their heads, whispering cutting words under their breath while I'm frog-marched through the airport corridors.

I hang my head. I don't have the courage to look them in the face like an innocent person should. Who will believe me anyway? They don't know me, so in my face, guilt and innocence merge. They're only relieved that people like me are kept away from them and their children. Tonight, they'll sleep a little easier.

○

The guards and I step outside. Night has fallen with a clang. I'm led to a minivan and told to climb into the back. They help me in, because my hands are bound. Both of them climb in with me and signal to the driver to pull off. I sit there for a moment getting my bearings, my eyes adjusting to the stifling dark inside. Then I turn to look through the grille. At least I'm anonymous in the dark, my features hidden by the shadows. And that's really all I long for now. To be nameless and insignificant.

People mill around the van, unaware of the soon-to-be jailbird inside. The engine starts and sets a slow rocking in motion as we make our way through the streets. I look at these two men, all three of us cramped into the same small space. We can't be more different in this moment. They fire away in Thai, laughing raucously, nodding their heads excitedly, their conversation comfortable, their words animated. They're probably sharing stories about their wives or girlfriends, chatting about their children's mischief. I sit between them in silence, my unborn baby imprisoned in my womb. If I go to jail for any length of time, what life, what future will my child have? I'm suddenly gripped by a bitter hatred for these men with their sunny faces and childish laughter. I wish they'd shut up! I cover my eyes to shut out the flashing neon lights of Bangkok that spangle the grille.

When the van stops, the guards open the doors and take hold of me. I step off the van and look up to see a small building. Its doors are secured with a thick chain that curls, python-like, round the handles. It looks nothing like a police station to me. The gloomy lighting gives off a depressing glow. Like an old, deserted prison – the kind that swallows human beings and spits out their bones. I shudder at the thought of what might happen to me in here.

But once inside, the lights are switched on and the floating darkness dissolves. Bunk beds and office desks sit side by side. My bags have travelled with me and one man now puts them down. "You sleep here. I sleep here." He points to a bunk bed, then himself and me in turn, smiling suggestively. There's a TV there, and the men scratch around till they find some videos and put them on. Naked, writhing bodies suddenly fill the screen. Asian porn. I'm terrified they'll both rape me. But for some reason, they're distracted by the clothing in my bags. And like kids raiding their parents' wardrobes for all the delicious adult fashions they can find, these two start trying on some of the clothes.

Then they remember I'm there. They look at me seductively, saying "*Suai, suai*!" (You're pretty!) And just as fear fills me again, another man dressed in white arrives. He must be their superior. He speaks to them harshly, and although I don't understand a word he says, it's clear he's angry with them. He walks up to me and addresses me in perfect English. He asks me what's happened, and I tell my story as best I can, keeping my emotions in check. He listens quietly as I beg him to find Jackson and Obey and arrest them. But he's surprised at my naivety. "Vanessa, they all go by those names. Those are not their real names. I'm afraid we won't be able to find them." I'm crushed to hear him say this. He tries to get me to eat something. But I can't. I have no appetite.

The holding cells will be my first taste of prison. But I have a choice. The man in white says, "Down in the basement, there are lots of foreign men locked up. They're big guys. You can sleep there, but if you feel safer, you can sleep up here in a bed." After what I've seen this evening, I'll take my chances with the foreigners – even if they are accused of being criminals. He leads me down a dark passageway, where the stench of sweat and urine stir the humid air. This is where the cells are housed. I have to be careful not to lose my footing because it's so dark in here; I can barely see where I'm going. I manage to make out a table on my right and see the outline of the cells on the left where the men are being kept.

He leaves me just beyond the threshold of a cell, the clatter of keys against metal bars behind me. His footsteps disappear up the dark passage, while I take in the barrenness of the cell. It's completely empty, except for a wooden door leading to a room with a hole in the floor that serves as the toilet. I look around for a tap where I can wash my hands, my face. There is none. In one corner, on the concrete floor, there's a bucket and pipe. And there, swarming around them are the only companions I'll have in this cell. Flying cockroaches and small lizards scurrying, clambering, not the least bit threatened by me. I slam the wooden door open, landing on my knees and vomiting again, even though my body has nothing more to expel.

I shut the door and sit down on the wooden floor of my cell, hugging my knees to my chest, crying quietly as I rock back and forth. "Come closer," I hear a man say. His voice is deep. Gentle. Definitely African-American. I'm still too afraid to answer. I shake my head. "Don't be scared. I just want to give you a mat and a pillow." Those are my first gifts as a prisoner. He tells me his name is Johnny as he pushes the mat and pillow through the bars toward me. Then he backs away.

In the few days and nights that follow, Johnny wins my trust. He's a faceless shadow, a stranger, but one I feel I can trust. "If you lie near the bars," he tells me on that first night, "I'll sleep close by on the other side. The guards come in and rape women at night. But I can fight them through the bars if you're close by. Don't sleep in the other room. I won't be able to do anything if they get you alone in there." I don't know if this cell holding Johnny and the other men is locked, or whether they can get out and attack me too. But I choose to believe Johnny. He seems like someone who'll look out for me in this hostile place for as long as I'm here. I make my bed close to the bars and feel Johnny's body radiate its heat from the other side. And no one touches me throughout that time.

I find myself opening up to Johnny. He's easy to talk to and he listens without judging me. I push a picture of Felix through the bars and tell him I'm carrying Felix's child. As I talk the tears come, hot, unrelenting. They blur my eyes and flood my face. I don't bother wiping them away. "Don't cry so much," Johnny says. "Something will happen to the baby. Just take it easy and be strong. Everything will be okay." I'm fine for a while, then I hear the roar of an aeroplane above our heads. And every few minutes, the thunder of those turbines reminds me that I don't belong here. I should be somewhere up in those skies, tucked among the load of human cargo, destined for South Africa.

At the holding cells, I pass some time by talking to Johnny and his friend. But most of all, I stare for hours, transfixed at the bars, picturing Felix barging in, demanding my release. I play and re-play the scene in my head. The Thai authorities with their big mouths and shit-brown uniforms cowering at the sound of his voice, while I walk out free, spitting in the face of their cruel justice system that wanted to turn me into human fodder.

But Felix never comes. Day after day, I sit there with these strangers-turned-friends who are prepared to spend their last bit of money on decent food for me. It means I can avoid the nauseating slop given to me, like over-boiled rice and pig's ear or some other pork off-cut. Johnny bribes the guards to bring me fruit and fried chicken. If I'm really lucky, I end up with a boiled duck's egg.

Johnny's also the reason I laugh again. He tells the guards to bring me a bag of food one day. I'm starving! I stick my hand inside with great anticipation and pull out something spiky. Not being able to see well in the dark, it almost feels like I'm holding a wriggling hedgehog in my hand. I get such a fright that I let out a yell and throw it across the cell. Johnny laughs till the tears stream down his face. The "hedgehog" turns out to be a prickly, long-haired fruit the Thais call *nok* – much like a litchi. He never lets me live that one down.

On my fourth day in those cells, they handcuff Johnny and take him away. He wears a blue-and-white tracksuit. I'm so upset. I'm losing a friend and a man who's protected me. But he tells me not to cry. "I promise I'll look for you, Vanessa. I think we're going to prisons in the same compound. I think you may be going to Lard Yao. I'm going to Klong Prem. Stay strong, Vanessa." As the officer pushes him out of the door, he calls out, "I promise to look for you. Everything will be okay."

I never see Johnny again. Thailand's prison system is so large, so complex, so full of tiny human cogs, that contact is fleeting. Someone briefly touches your life and moves on. But while he's jailed in Klong Prem, Johnny finds me through the embassy and writes to me. After he's released, he still wants to stay in contact, but it doesn't feel right. When you walk out of a place like this, you have to leave the nightmare behind or it destroys you.

When Johnny leaves, the holding cells become unbearable for me. At night, thoughts of home haunt me. I still don't know whether I will be free again or will die in this country.

Most of all, I wonder what happened the night Felix came to the airport and waited for me and I never got off that plane. I see him standing there, bewildered. Scanning every face. Looking at the clocks. Watching the hours die. The wilted bouquet in one hand losing its petals as he walks away. Is he pestering the authorities for information? Does he know what's happened to me, where I'm being kept? And will he come to save me?

And while the thoughts and doubts and questions swarm in my head, a hundred mosquitoes wage war on my body every night. They attack almost every ounce of my exposed flesh. And each morning I'm full of fresh ripe red blotches that slowly change the landscape of my skin. At first I swat them away. But after a few days I don't care. I don't care how I look either. Me, the ramp model. I was once so conscious of every detail of my appearance, matching all my outfits perfectly. Never leaving the house without make-up on. And now I have no urge to shower or comb my hair until Johnny stuck the hose through the bars and I had my first cold shower. I open the toilet door at an angle, hide myself and change my clothes there.

It's hard to care since Johnny's left. He gave me shorts and a T-shirt and made sure the guards bought a mosquito repellent coil for us to burn at night. But without his constant motivation, I fall into a deep lethargy, every moment, every thought, every movement draining my last reserves. And something I witness the day Johnny goes, leaves me shocked. I see the guards handing out slips to some of the inmates. And when I ask why they're doing this, Johnny's friend tells me the guards are selling heroin back to some of the prisoners who were caught with it. The same men who have locked me up for drug smuggling have become dealers themselves! This is such a blow to me. What hope do I have of pleading my innocence, of fleeing this place, if the system is so rotten from the inside? The authorities might turn a blind eye to their own people breaking the law, but I doubted they would ever let me go unpunished for the same crime.

CHAPTER 4

Court

27 April, 1994. The day I go to court, hands cuffed, head bowed in shame, while millions of my fellow South Africans are lining up in queues kilometres long, full of pride and excitement. They'll go to the ballot boxes to place their marks there, electing the world's most famous prisoner – Nelson Mandela, a man whose walk to freedom has been long and painful. How I yearn for the smell of my country's soil. How I long to see the faces of my people and hear their unique voices.

I remember the look in the eyes of ordinary people before I left. They seemed taller, prouder, eager to live in this new democracy, after our country came so close to civil war but chose to solve its problems by talking. The hand Nelson Mandela has extended is to people of all colours, people from all walks of life. And it reminds us that even if it takes years, justice can come. You can close your eyes to a land of inequality one night and wake up to a completely different country in the morning. Our political prisoners have been freed. And it shows the world that we are a people who fight for justice, who value human rights.

But here in Thailand, the picture is so different. My seven days in the holding cells have expired. It's time for me to go before a Thai judge and plead my case. I dress myself in an outfit that I think looks right for court – it's the best I can do: blue-and-white striped dungarees and sandals. I try to make myself look as decent as possible considering what I have, braiding my hair into two neat plaits. The last time I'd had my picture taken was for the Miss South Africa semi-finals, supposed to take place later this year. I spent hours finding the right outfits, shopping for the most flattering costume for the swimsuit section. Searching for a suit cut for my body. But on this day that all feels like pure vanity. And that memory is so distant; none of it seems to matter anymore.

Transported by the Thai police to have my mug shot taken – the one that will appear on my criminal record – I enter a room with a white board on the back wall and take my place against it. I want to cry when they hand me a clipboard with my name on it. But I hold it up. They instruct me to turn to the left and then to the right. Out of the corner of each eye, I see the flash. But when I turn to face that camera head-on, it hits me so hard. I feel like a criminal. And the shame washes over me while the lens refocuses to find the detail of my face. This face I've greeted in the mirror each morning, that Felix has planted his sensual kisses on, the face my mother's adored since her eyes fell on me as a baby – how easily it becomes the face of a criminal. The camera clicks and records that moment, freezes it in time so no one will forget, especially not me.

I walk away, dazed, into the open door of a waiting police car. Its sirens blare, parting traffic, turning the heads of pedestrians as we make our way to the court. It's an imposing building with white-tiled floors and a long hallway. In large cells lining the walls on my right I pass men, shackled like animals in cages, their hands and feet chained. I'm afraid to look them in the eye. Afraid to see my own pain mirrored in those unkempt faces. But I do anyway. I'm looking out for Johnny, hoping to have one proper glimpse of him in the light. But he isn't with those men.

The police escorts and I finally reach the courtroom at the end of that elastic hallway. The Thai courtrooms are unlike ours. Here, the accused sits in a chair placed right at the front of this large room, in full view of the magistrate who speaks to the court, but more directly to the suspect. When the magistrate comes in, he asks me to stand. Then he begins reading a long judgment, all of it in Thai. I understand none of it, except my mangled name. Vanessa Leone Goosen becomes "Wanessa Lay-on Goose-in". I'm made to stand each time he calls my name.

I study the magistrate's face. It's completely neutral. His voice, too, hides the seriousness of his words. My mind wanders. I make up a version of his ruling in my head in which he says I've been wrongfully accused and I must be allowed to go free. But there are very few magistrates in Thailand who would dare defy the prime minister, whose war on drugs is being taken very seriously. When the magistrate stops talking, my daydream shatters. An official immediately brings me some court papers, my sworn testimony. He orders me to sign them, but they're all in Thai. So I refuse to sign the documents. I later find out that this wad of papers is a full confession in which I admit to being a drug trafficker, and say I tried to leave Bangkok with 1.7 kilograms of heroin stashed in books in my bag.

I ask the court official if the documents can be translated into English so I can read them. "Impossible!" he sneers. I have to stand my ground, even though I'm terrified. What if I end up pleading guilty, signing my life away? No. It's a chance I can't take. When he asks me once more, I again refuse. I'm told I have to leave the courtroom, no closer to understanding whether I've been thrown a lifeline or a noose.

Another official leads me through a small side door, down an aisle and into another, larger room. There are about thirty women there – foreign and Thai prisoners, all dressed in the same mud-brown uniforms. Only two other women, both Thai, are wearing civilian clothes like me. They look up at me as I'm brought in. And over the course of the day, the numbers swell gradually, the wheels of justice (or injustice) turning slowly but steadily.

Before I'm allowed in, I'm briefly searched for drugs. I barely step into the room when a young woman rushes up to me. The style of her bleached-blonde hair gives her a vaguely South African appearance. "I'm Elise," she says. And I immediately know she's from home. When she realises that I, too, am South African and can speak Afrikaans, she makes the strangest comment. "I'm glad you came. I prayed for a friend," she says. I'm not sure what she's expecting me to say but I'm taken aback by her careless words. She's the fly in the spider's web, stuck so fast, it knows it'll never break free. And so it prays for the next fly to land there and get stuck too, so they can be eaten together. I don't answer her. But it's not long before other foreign prisoners come over to share their stories with me.

The stories these women tell me leave me cold. One woman called Joy tells me she's been sentenced to life in prison. Yet another Ethiopian woman whispers that she's been given the death sentence. We're all accused of the same crime. I need to hear at least one story that ends differently, at least one that will give me just a shred of hope. But no one comes forward with that. And I become so distressed by what may lie ahead for me that the ground suddenly begins to shift under my feet and I almost feel it give way. Someone realises I'm about to pass out and shoves some pungent mint-scented salts under my nose. This keeps me from fainting.

The hours pass with the odd trickle of women into the room. We're left to wait there, in the heat, until the court closes at 4pm. Then, all the prisoners line up according to their numbers. At first, I'm not sure what's expected of me. I have no prison number, but then the guards call out my name and surname instead. It's confirmed. Wherever these women are headed to, I'm going with them.

I'm placed second-to-last in the line that files out onto the bus waiting outside. The ground is baking, like hot coals under our feet. Wire mesh barricades the windows of this bus, restricting our view. But that doesn't matter. No one's taking in the scenery. In that state of mind, the beauty of everything escapes me. That hour-long drive to the prison could be the longest journey of my life. The questions are buzzing around in my head, a swarm of flies laying their filthy larvae. *Where are they taking me? What's going to happen to me? Did they convict me of drug-smuggling? Am I being thrown into prison even though I didn't sign those papers? Are they taking me somewhere to kill me, or am I like that woman who got life in prison?* I'm guessing that they must have convicted me or I wouldn't be here.

As we drive past the men's prison, Klong Prem, I wonder how Johnny's doing and if our paths will ever cross again. But that thought's wiped quickly from my mind as I look up and my eyes fall on two massive gates, splashed with light blue paint – the colour of a baby's nursery. Fear digs its claws in deep. *Will my child be born in here? Will I ever see the world outside these gates again? My family? Felix?* I suddenly realise that these could be my last moments of freedom. Panicked, I spin my head round and desperately try to drink it all in – the streetlight, the cars, the leaves hanging lonely from the only tree I can see.

Just then, the prison gates scrape open, the grating sound of metal on concrete. The bus hurtles in. And when I turn to look back, the guards are tiny specks. Little plastic soldiers, shadowed against the vast backdrop of those metal gates that I know will swallow up women like me; will shred every fibre of us that can't be sent back home in a cheap wooden coffin varnished with our blood. The gates swing shut behind me. And still today that image is burnt into me. It lives beneath my eyelids when I'm trying to force myself to sleep. Because that's the moment I know that my country and my people and my dreams are shut away beyond those gates, so far out of my reach.

From now on, Lard Yao Prison is my new home.

CHAPTER 5

Body search

"Spread your legs!"

I am standing suspended over a chair, my arms gripping the back rest, my legs straddling both sides of it. My thighs are beginning to ache from this half-squat. Her swollen fingers are slithering under my brown skirt. Suddenly they thrust into me from underneath. "You're hurting me!" I cry out, as she probes, digs, violates me. But I get no reaction. She only stares blankly, small eyes buried in her large face, while her two calloused fingers, muscular, forked, jaggedly scour the walls of my vagina.

This skirt which I've already come to hate so much – reeking of the body odour of someone else – is the thin film that stands between me and complete nakedness. My upper body is bare, my chest exposed. I'm among the last in a human production line that's all bare flesh and wide-open mouths, jutting tongues, dangling breasts and parted legs. They search us with care. Invade every nook. Breach every cranny. They'll come to know us new arrivals intimately – each spot, each blemish, each fold.

Now it's dark, but that hides none of my shame. From the moment I got off that bus, I knew this wasn't a place anyone tries to escape. I look at the inmates who've been here for a while. They're resigned. They know not to protest. Not to complain. It could be worse. They could be standing in front of a firing squad instead of a warden with her fingers up their vagina. And that's why they submit from the moment the bus driver cuts the engine, and guides them through a small door to the second set of gates. That's why these grown women line up without question, like school children for roll call.

These women all address the wardens as "*Khun*", meaning "officer". "When the warden calls your name," one woman tells me, "you must say your surname because you do not have a prison number yet." I nod gratefully. I feel like a child in the presence of a Grade 1 teacher, who will give me a gold star if I do as I'm told. The list of names and numbers seems endless. Mine is the last to be called. "Wanessa!" the warden says. "Goosen…" I respond, none of the enthusiasm in my voice that the others show.

As darkness settles, we're led up to the last set of gates that gives way to the prison grounds. We line up outside the hospital building, single-file, the wardens in the lead. The old inmates need no cue. As soon as the procession stops, they start undressing. They meekly shed their clothes, an old habit. But I'm too ashamed to remove mine. They're already buck-naked, ready for their cavity searches. And I'm peeling my clothes off item by item, hesitantly – a clumsy stripper undressing with one hand, hiding her bare skin with the other.

This is how the guards make sure that after every court outing, we come back without drugs or weapons stuck up our holes. The wardens go about their work like they're sorting sirloin from offal in a meat factory. The hunks of meat in front of them aren't human beings anymore. They pinch large tracts of flesh between their fingers, grope their way along thighs, scratch around in armpits and ears, prise apart fingers and toes or lift breasts to see what's underneath them. Fingers, stiff as pokers, look for the presence of drugs under tongues, scrape the plump insides of cheeks for any trace. False nails are ripped off, hair extensions are massacred.

I wince at the mention of my name. I haven't been quick enough to undress. And the officer holding up the diarrhoea-brown skirt meant for me is growing impatient. Her colleague is barking orders at me, looking on in scorn while my panties fall to the floor and the jewellery melts off my hands.

"Open mouth!" she shouts in a high-pitched voice. Her fingers yank at my tongue, drill into my gums, almost cause me to gag as they lengthen down the back of my throat. My eyes are shut. Maybe it'll be easier if I can't see her huge hands looming. "Loosen hair!" My thick, curly mop falls out in all directions. Her fingers get stuck in it. Frustrated, she breaks through the knots as I yelp in pain. Her fingernails scratch at my scalp. My breasts are young and pert. She knows I can't hide anything under them but she still jabs at them for fun. She tells me to part my legs – Part One of The Vaginal Examination. Rough and indifferent, she grabs at me superficially, finds nothing there. "Tie skirt and go room," she orders, and calls out to the prisoner behind me.

That's how I've come to be here. In this small room with one chair in the corner that I've been squatting over since I came in. My eyes are beginning to water from the pain. I'm swallowing hard, forcing my tears backwards so they don't come pouring out of me as she prods. This woman feels nothing for me. But I can't help it. Again I say, "You're hurting me!" – slightly more forcefully this time. She parts her lips to reveal jutting teeth that look poised to jump out of her mouth. She laughs. "*Mai-pie-laai*!" (Never mind!) she says. I grit my teeth and silently curse her. *You bitch! Bloody bitch with steelwool hair standing up like black straw around your ugly face! You made me cry!* And yet, she's one of us. An ordinary prison rat, so proud of the power she has to poke around in our private parts.

When she finds nothing, the wardens lead me to the back of the building. It's dark, but in the moonlight I can see a large rectangular trough ahead of me, like the one animals drink out of. The moon's reflection plays inside it, silver, shimmering like lit tungsten. Someone shoves a bowl into my hands and says, "Shower. Shower." I raise my leg, thinking I must climb into the trough but when the others see me about to plunge in, they say "No, no! Use bowl. Shower, use bowl."

A Thai girl shows me how to remove the thick brown skirt

and wash. I'm meant to drench my whole body with the filthy contents of this trough, drawn bowl by bowl. I take the skirt off, happy to be rid of the stench of perspiration that stains it. But then I'm naked and embarrassed again. Carrying out this private duty to myself in full view of others. There's no soap. But I begin to pour the water over myself. It makes me shiver. I pour more and more, the filling, the emptying becoming more frenzied each time. I splash it over my head, so the flow takes my silent tears with it.

But it's not enough to dampen what is stirring inside me. A smouldering anger that rises up, unexpected and volcanic and raw. Rage like I've never allowed myself to feel since my arrest, believing that someone – the man I love – will at least come to my rescue. But days have gone and I'm seething at his silence. *Where is he?* Where was he when those bastards interrogated me and took me away in handcuffs? Where was he when I lay on the floor of a holding cell, the mosquitoes eating me alive? And where is he now that I am standing here, naked and humiliated, pouring bowl after bowl of filthy water on myself, feeling its grit fasten to my skin? Has he spent the last seven days bathing in luxury, eating the best food, sleeping in his own comfortable bed, knowing that everything has changed so drastically for me? "Fuck you, Felix! Fuck you! I hate you for leaving me here!" The more I scream the more I want to scream. "I hate you! I hate you, Felix!... *I hate you!*" I crumple into a sopping heap on the cement next to the trough, still screaming my anger at him.

Some Thai girls come running to me. "*Pen-arai?*" (What's wrong?) I recoil. "Don't fucking touch me! Don't you fucking touch me!" I snarl at them. They're taken aback. One of the girls runs off to call the same woman who's just penetrated me with her lumpy fingers in the hospital room. My rage is so intense, so uncontrollable that I cannot calm it. I prepare to turn it on her. I spin around to face her, a rabid look in my eyes. I will scratch her eyes out! Rip every last bristle of hair off her fucking head!

But she suddenly bends down and sits next to me, a look of genuine sensitivity in her eyes. I don't understand. *Isn't this the same bitch who hurt me just a few minutes ago? Took pleasure in it?* Now, she sits here, comforting me in her broken English. Finding the kindest words in her small vocabulary to soothe me. She discourages me from lying naked on the cement, saying it's no good for the baby. Then she throws her arms around me and holds me as the sobs rack my body. "I know you not want be here. I also want you go home because you young and this not your country. You angry, I know, with someone bring you inside here. But you must think about baby."

She rocks me in her arms and allows me a moment of release, when all my pent-up rage dissolves into tears. I'm weirdly comforted by this strange woman's embrace. This tough-love prisoner digging deep to find the memory of her first days here before she became Cavity Queen. She allows time to stand still for me. It doesn't matter that Lard Yao is still spinning around me, hordes of women caught up in its orbit. There's a moment for me to stop and grieve the loss of my freedom. To begin swallowing that first taste of bitterness that comes with a frightening new life, away from the life that used to be mine. After a time, a sense of calm comes over me. And when I look at her again, the hardness I saw in her face in the hospital has thawed, leaving behind an air of sincerity and grace. "They're not my books. I promise. No one wants to believe me but they are not my books. I just want to go home." She hugs me tighter. "Tomorrow I contact embassy, then they contact family for you," she says.

I clamber back onto my feet and finish cleaning myself up. They allow me to fetch my toiletry bag and underwear from my luggage. I'm given a locker in which to keep my things, but no lock to ensure none of it is stolen. It doesn't matter to me anyway. I shove my belongings inside. I don't care whether I'll see them again. Then a guard and a prisoner take me to a room on the top floor of Paitoon Building. This is where I'll sleep. There are a few hospital beds in the room, occupied by older women. The younger ones sit on the floor.

Before I'm allowed in, a nurse again searches me for the presence of drugs or weapons. When she's satisfied that nothing's passed her hawk eyes, she hands me a big towel. I wait for a blanket too but there's no such luxury available. She points to the towel. "This for sleep on."

"Which bed am I sleeping in?" I ask her. She smirks. "No bed. You sleep on floor," she says. "People on bed here twenty-five year!" The warden gives me another brown prison uniform saying, "This one extra," and she leaves. I fold my towel three times and mark out my tiny patch of floor. It's about the size of 2½ floor tiles. And I know my long legs will be cramped in here, will have to touch the legs of these women I don't know.

Pie Ratana is full of questions. She's known as the *mayhong* of the room, which puts her in charge. I tell her my name, surname, nationality and that I'm pregnant. She writes it down. She assists the wardens with efficiency, always clutching her clipboard and notebook. Having Pie Ratana as our *mayhong* has its advantages. Because she has a foreign husband, she can speak fluent English. I talk to her and ask her how old my fellow inmates are.

Many are over fifty. I imagine them coming here as I have, scatter-brained twenty-something-year-olds, full of optimism that every court hearing will bring them one step closer to freedom. But for them, the years have piled up on each other, carved these women's faces with furrows so deep, you could almost map their journey – its peaks, its slumps – to this moment. Their uniforms are branded with a white star that makes them appear strangely disposable, like Jews in Nazi Germany on the brink of a gas chamber – except they're not.

They wear their badges with pride in this place that rewards survival, that bets on those who dodge the executioner's gun. And they've done exactly that, in a country that will happily spray bullets at convicts like a can of Doom at flies. They have something in their eyes I don't. An acceptance of their situation. Perhaps it's hard-won after twenty-five years in here. I hope I never find out.

I'm one of the newcomers who claims a sleeping area near the toilet in one corner of the room. I lie there, trying to fend off the heat that's grown unbearable. It seems to rush at me from every direction. And the ceiling fans overhead only seem to circulate the suffocating air. At times it's hard to breathe. It doesn't help that the toilet we're squashed against is a yawning, stinking hole, crawling with the bacteria of all those brave enough to squat over it. At first I can't – not in this cell full of other women. There's no door. There are only two metre-high walls surrounding it, so that we climb in and hunker down when the urge grabs us, while the sounds of our pissing and shitting fill our fellow inmates' ears.

A Chinese woman casually strips off her clothes and bra and lies next to me. She'll sleep in the nude tonight. This isn't something I'll ever be able to do as long as I'm surrounded by complete strangers. Here again, as I lay my head on the towel, in the distance, I pick up the roar of jet engines. And although I allowed this to tear me apart in the holding cells, tonight it feels like a springboard to get myself out of here. Each time I'm tortured by this reminder of home, I repeat a mantra to myself. *You don't belong here, Vanessa. You will go home.*

Night never brings any peace though, because the cement floors are so cold and the blinding fluorescent lights burn day and night – a subtle reminder that at Lard Yao, everything is seen, every moment of every day. That first night, I lie curled up in the membrane of my towel like a foetus, floating on the breaths of all the women around me exhaling their pain. I tuck my arm underneath my head, a scrawny pillow, willing myself to sleep. *Things will be better in the morning.* In my head, it can all be fixed – the suffering of previous days erased, my criminal record scrubbed clean, my leap onto a flight straight home. But my heart knows this would be too easy. There's a reason people fear the Thai justice system so much. Sometimes, the gap between the law and justice is so big. And tonight I know I'm hanging by my nails, in the space between.

CHAPTER 6

Lard Yao

My first morning in Lard Yao, my eyes split open to find the dark still hanging heavy at the window. There's a dull hum in the distance, like the sound of food being prepared in a kitchen. Every now and then, I hear the muffled clang of a pot or the tinkle of falling cutlery. But inside this cell, there's only the chorus of deep breathing, like the sea rush you hear when a shell's clamped to your ear.

The fluorescent bulb still casts its glare. But I pretend that the dark from outside has flooded in. I pull myself up as quietly as I can, and begin my walk barefoot to the toilet, navigating between the twist of bodies on the floor. Shit! I don't have any toilet paper. But I can't hold it in any longer. My bladder is aching from waiting this long. I swallow hard, squat and relieve myself. I rinse myself with a communal bowl, hoping the echo of it doesn't wake anyone. But they're all wound too tightly into their dreams to hear.

I creep back to my spot on the floor just before the wardens wake us, their shrill, nasal voices piercing the new daylight. Bleary-eyed, I'm unstable on my feet, while the other inmates spring into action, folding their blankets, packing up their belongings like this is a drill. And once the wardens unlock the doors, I'm washed away in a shoal of bodies, metal containers and yellow plastic bowls bobbing on the surface. In the mad dash, people fall over and injure themselves. But no one stops to help them. I panic. I have no idea where I'm going. I look around to see if anyone might be willing to help me. And then, in that ocean of faces, Elise surfaces – my spider's nest companion – and I suddenly feel, despite my first reaction to her, that I'm being saved by this woman who prayed me into coming here.

"Hurry!" she says. "We only have forty-five minutes to shower, get dressed and eat. We have to be ready to work by eight, and for fifteen minutes before that, we sing the King's Song. Come on, let's go!" Her words are breathless. We're both washed up on the shores of the trough that somehow looks a lot less threatening than it did last night. It's about five metres long and seventy centimetres high, a detachable tap at one end. We line up. I watch the others and copy them. They brush their teeth with one hand and shampoo their hair with the other. An officer then fills the trough and we line up around it. The prisoners in charge count, "One, two, three." And with each number, we raise one bowl of water and throw it over ourselves. They ask, "is everybody ready?" Then they count from four to fifteen and by that time, we have to have washed ourselves clean.

When I get back, I find that my extra uniform's been stolen. But there's no time to dwell on it, because the tsunami of bodies is gathering again. I'm shoved forward among these starving women towards breakfast in a drab face-brick building called the *gong li un*. I'm quite proud of myself at this moment, coping with the strangeness of all of this, until I allow myself one fleeting thought of Felix. He's suddenly there – standing right in front of me, beaming, tray in hand – breakfast in bed. And I am shooing him away playfully. *You know I can't eat this now because of my morning sickness.*

I'm so wounded by the image of Felix I've just allowed to be let loose in my mind. I'm starting to learn that thoughts of him no longer lift me. They only remind me of the devastating turn my life has taken. I must be more careful in future. Control my thoughts, so this stay will become more bearable. The women around me are fighting their way to the front of this line. Without money I can't buy anything. But Elise knows this. She splashes out on peanut butter sandwiches and Lipton Ice Tea for the both of us. In this hellhole, it's truly a feast!

Elise offers me a guided tour of Lard Yao, like it's a top-class resort. The prison buildings are u-shaped. On the right arm, there's an entrance to the prison for foreign visitors, a lawyers' room, the embassy room and the hospital, which contains the mother's room and the nursery building. I'm just over three months pregnant now. Elise is pregnant too. And I wonder how long it'll be before we're sent there. Next to that are the four buildings where the inmates sleep.

On the opposite side are four factories where the prisoners work. The prison uniforms for both Klong Prem and Lard Yao are made in the first factory. The others make children's clothes and army uniforms. Elise tells me that in each of these factories I could find work cutting off the loose threads hanging from the garments to neaten them, or assemble packages for airline passengers on long-haul flights. There's even a hair salon, a massage parlour and a restaurant staffed by inmates.

We go past the prison school with a library on the second floor, and the buildings that form the bottom of the 'u', including the flower factory, bakery and the home *pradict* (another factory where prisoners make sarongs and dyed material). Elise tells me the *lanka* is similar to a convenience store where you can buy anything from milk and sugar to padlocks. The flower factory, the *dok mai*, is where artificial flowers are made to be sold to the public. Similarly, in *cheum chom*, meals are cooked for public consumption. Lard Yao is a unique money-making machine. The prisoners work for almost nothing, but Elise tells me the prison officials make lots of money.

The King's Song suddenly bursts out of speakers nearby. Everyone, no matter what they're doing, stands deathly still. I want to lean over to ask Elise why everyone's so quiet when I see that she, too, has turned into a statue and is staring straight ahead. Frozen there, only their mouths moving, the women begin to sing, *"Akara sielapien klongsat kandontee..."* First, I keep quiet because

I don't know the words. But I'm afraid the wardens will punish me for not singing along. So I mimic the sounds as best I can, trying to mouth these foreign words that weave and loop around my tongue as though they'll knot it. When it becomes too much, I hum, which I think is fine for a new arrival. When it's finished, Elise tells me we were singing in honour of Thailand's king, Bhumibol Adulyadej, whom the Thais revere like a god. They sing this twice a day. Elise doesn't know what the words mean either.

Despite hating what's happened, in the days that follow I try to adapt to this new environment, just to move forward. I'm learning the routine, showing respect for the authorities. I hope my good behaviour will count in my favour when I go before the courts, begging them to release me. But I'm also emotionally spent. I've had almost no time to deal with what's happened to me. And the strain is beginning to tell on me. I'm feeling disorientated. I fight it, but my body's tired. I haven't slept properly for several nights and my thoughts are scrambled. I'm so scared because I still don't know whether I'll die in this country or be forced to live out the rest of my life here. And the faces of Felix, my mother and sisters, my darling Aunt Rushda, float in and out of my thoughts. I'm desperate to let them know where I am, but I just don't know how.

My second afternoon at Lard Yao, I'm pulled out of my body as though I'm watching everything from above. I'm here among these crowds of women, but I'm also standing at a window looking in on them. My sense of reality is dissolving like a block of ice in boiling water. And when I close my eyes to force my thoughts together, there are suddenly shards under my eyelids, piercing them, cutting them. Thousands of disjointed fragments of the last few days. Splinters of my life, my trauma, all carelessly stuck together to remind me: there's no escaping this hell I have landed up in.

And suddenly everything picks up speed. I'm unsteady on my feet. Lard Yao is spinning so fast, I feel it wants to throw me off like some demented Ferris wheel. People are hurtling at me, bombarding me with a million questions and rules and instructions, all at the same time. I'm trying to understand. Trying to make out what they're saying. But the voices are too many and too loud. I'm blinded by so many women flying at me like bugs onto a windscreen – Asian women, white women, short women, dreadlocked women, asking me everything, demanding to know all of me – my whole life in one day. What's your name? Where do you come from? How did you get locked up here? Did you get life? Did you get the death sentence? Are you pregnant? Are you *mulato*? Are you black? Are you South African?

I'm human! I'm just human!

And then I'm having a pregnancy test, gushing on a stick to prove I deserve a spot in the mother's wing. And it's five days before the results will come back. I'm praying. I'm hoping. Desperate for time to fast-forward five days just so I can leave this crowded cell and move to the mother's section and watch these thronging faces evaporate. I throw myself on the floor that night and sleep comes, drenching me in restless nightmares. But at least the day's sounds begin to die around me. The oppressive heat stands still. I hear Lard Yao screeching to a slow rotation, metal on metal. I fill my lungs with the prison air that makes me feel strangely drunk. But at least I can breathe again.

On my third night there, I look up and there's a new prisoner standing in front of us. She looks lost and untidy. A pair of shabby-looking pyjamas hang off her frame. But her face is familiar, so I look closer. And my mind suddenly jumps backwards. Victoria? I'm sucked back to Don Muang Airport. To the vision of this young, hip woman with a heavy American accent, decked out in her expensive cream suit that'd take me years to save up to buy. She's just got off the same flight as me. And as she drops an envelope, I bend to pick it up and we introduce ourselves.

In the taxi heading to my hotel, I admire her sassy, stylish African-American style. She doesn't have any change though, so I pay for the trip. In the coming days, Victoria and I sit in my sweltering hotel room, eat the worst food we've ever tasted, laugh raucously about the creepy men in this dingy hotel and drink too much beer that makes us clown around. I tell her all about Felix and the baby. She seems genuinely happy for me.

And when we hit the streets, Victoria guides me through the

offerings at Bangkok's Pratunum Market where fabrics hang dripping with colour – delicious gashes of scarlet, turquoise, emerald green, the pigment so intense the fabric throbs beneath it. She's vibrant, electrifying the pavement she walks on.

And now Victoria stands before me. The light in her eyes is dim in this jail cell. She's pale.

"What are you doing here?" We mirror each others' words. She's lost the vibrancy in her voice. She speaks softly now, timidly, the glitz of her American accent gone. She sounds like me. And I can't bring myself to ask her what she's in for or to trust her anymore. She speaks vaguely about her situation. And she walks away, her steps careless and clumsy. So different to the confident woman I walked alongside on the streets of Bangkok.

Victoria and I have nothing more to say about this short "past life" in which we knew each other. There's no mention of the two of us, caught up in the excitement of Songkrang, the Thai New Year celebrations, shrieking with laughter, spraying each other with water. In these walls, everything that came before somehow seems imagined anyway. But I do wonder whether it really was a coincidence that we met. What are the chances that a woman who spent so much time with me in Bangkok and I have ended up in the same jail, charged with the same crime?

A week passes. Then two weeks. And every twelve days, I'm hauled off to court for an exhausting repeat of my first appearance before the judge. Nothing changes. Prison to bus to court to bus to prison. A smudge of words and gestures I still don't understand. What the hell are they waiting for? Maybe they're trying to wear me down so I'll give up and sign their confession. Otherwise, what joy does this judge get out of staring down through bulging eyes at this woman, just twenty-one years old, who sits there, dumb, because she doesn't understand a word that falls from his mouth? When I get back, no one says anything to me. So I can't have got the death sentence yet.

But one night after I've appeared in court and returned to Lard Yao, the officer on duty falls asleep and leaves the TV on in our cell. And they're televising the actual execution of a Thai prisoner. It takes a while for me to figure out this is real. There's a small house with a crowd of people standing outside. And then he appears, this nameless man, in his handcuffs. He's taken inside and his eyes are covered with a cloth, which hides the fear in them. In front, there's a black curtain with a heart painted on it. And when the curtain is drawn, there's a small piece of wood behind it, a seat jutting out of the wall. They calmly place him on it. The curtain is closed. And the executioner takes aim directly into the middle of that heart on the curtain. There's a flash of gunfire and a thud as he hits the floor. I'm terrified. And as I lie there, the concrete burrowing into my bones, I suddenly realise how much higher the stakes have become. Just a few weeks ago, I was fighting to stay out of jail. Now, I'm fighting to stay alive.

CHAPTER 7

Memories of home

I'm longing for just one full night of sleep at Lard Yao. I lie awake for hours, tossing on my tiny patch of floor, when sleep suddenly looms over me, dragging me into the most vivid dreams of home. There's such release in those dreams. I'm safe. Completely at peace. Reunited with the people who own my heart. I scream, I cry with joy at the fierceness with which I pull them into me and stay there, bolted tightly into their arms.

"Wake up! Time to wake up!" And suddenly something is pulling me away from them, like the force of a sea current, sweeping me backwards. The lights are stabbing my eyes from above. And I can't tell whether it's blood or tears streaming out of them. I feel like I've been shipwrecked on Lard Yao; that these bodies moving about me are imagined and I'm really completely alone. But if I don't get up and move with the tide, I'll be drowned. I struggle to my feet and try to orientate myself. I'm battling to focus. As I stand at the trough throwing water on myself, the taste of my family is too sweet in my mouth to eat for days. I don't belong here. I don't deserve this.

I want my old life back – my life that begins at our family home in Canoncross Road, Carston, Port Elizabeth. 18 December 1972. A private nursing sister eases me into the world, a tiny, milk-scented bundle handed to my family just a week before Christmas.

I'm the second of two girls my mother feels she reached into the sky for, and plucked straight out of heaven. My brother, Marlon, slap-bang in the middle of us, sits like a thorn among roses.

The three of us are happy children – a dollop of honey in the well of bitterness that is my mother's life. A life soured by the violence of my father Leon. My mother Minah marries him as a naïve nineteen-year-old, in the flush of love. She's taken with his exotic heritage – half-German, half-Chinese, but he's still only a boy really, at the age of twenty-one. My mother is beautiful. And it's a mystery my father never succeeds in destroying that beauty, because he certainly tries hard. He's never happy with the perfection of it. Never satisfied that he's the guy who ended up with the ringside seat, close enough to admire it everyday. He has to control it. He has to punish her for it. With time, his jealousy and possessiveness grow. She's a prisoner in our house, forbidden to socialise, see her friends, go to a party once in a while. She lives in fear of him. But she also believes you accept the consequences of your actions. And she chose him.

When I'm barely three months old, my father is wiped out in a car accident. Quick and final. Erased from our lives like a mistake in a spelling test. It's expected to unleash grief on our household, but my mother doesn't know what to feel. Part of her is sad he had to die that way. The rest is relieved he's gone. As he lies there in the coffin, cold and bruised, she mourns the man who first fell in love with her, who promised to love her till his last breath. But she's angry at the man who threw her against walls and smashed his fist into her face. She grieves more for the confident, happy woman she used to be, now lying in the coffin next to him.

Marlon and I know nothing. He's three years old and too young to understand. I'll have no memory at all of my father, and learn his face in pictures only. But my sister Jacky – she's been a silent witness. A sad, frightened, crumbling witness to the brutal war my father's waged against my mother. A war of bare knuckles and splintered bones, of bloody noses, split lips and pleas for mercy. On the outside, Jacky is well built, sturdy almost. She's the girl who falls and gets up without crying or rubbing her knees. Pain is a numb word in her five-year-old child-vocabulary. She stands and watches each time. A lonely spectator in a game with a set of rules only my parents understand. When my father dunks my mother's head into the wall like a basketball, Jacky is watching. When he smudges my mother's body blue and black with welts like crude kiddy paintings, Jacky is watching. When he leaves her in a heap on the floor, like a pile of dirty laundry he steps on, Jacky is watching. Jacky's mind overflows – a dam without sluice gates. It bursts its sides in one horrific explosion when she's twelve years old. And we spend the years that follow trying to find our sister buried beneath the debris.

In prison, Jacky's face always looms before me. Her liquid brown eyes. The avalanche of long black hair over her shoulders – innocent strands woven into a silky noose she tries to strangle herself with after my father's death. Some days she screams uncontrollably, claiming to see my father. She sleepwalks at night. In the day, she flings open the door and barrels down the street, my mother, my uncles, the darting eyes of curious neighbours, following her, while she chases my father's ghost. Jacky cries endlessly. She sits with a pair of sharp scissors and shreds her clothes, until only a mound of ragged threads remain. And one day, she lifts a glass to the light and likes the reflections playing there. And she suddenly lets it go, lets it shatter to the ground. Then she steps, barefoot, into the glinting pool below, dancing in its shards that slash her skin, embed themselves in it. An underfoot mosaic, purple with her blood.

Jacky is a child. Even as an adult, she remains that five-year-old girl, looking in on the horrors of this place called adulthood, stepping on the threshold of it but never going in. She speaks like a child. She acts like a child. She's been institutionalised several times. She's never had a job. My mother takes care of Jacky, her daughter-sapling pruned by harsh life into a fragile bonsai. And that's why, even though I'm younger, I always try to protect Jacky from herself and anyone I think might hurt her. How will I do that now? And how much more damage will my imprisonment cause?

A few years after my father dies, my mother marries again and

Elton and Melissa are born. Melissa, now a teenager, is a delight. She'll help my mother with Jacky whenever she needs it. But Melissa is just a girl. And I know it's unfair that she should carry this burden. This is the curse of the Goosen children. We're either kids, forced into adulthood early, or adults who can never move beyond being children.

I miss my family terribly and long for any contact from home. Day after day, I see the prison mail being sorted and I wonder if somewhere in that pile, there are just a few words of hope for me. The others rush up to receive their letters from home, while I stay sitting, forgotten. I console myself with the thought that if they haven't written to me, they haven't yet managed to find out where I am.

Then, in early May, a peach envelope arrives at Lard Yao. It's addressed to me. I scream with delight! It's in the handwriting of my close childhood friend, Christine. She's found me! I cry when I see her name on the back of the envelope. This letter is gold to me. I rip it open. My heart is pummelling in my chest. And there, inside is a letter in Afrikaans:

> *Dear Vanessa, I hope you are fine and I want you to know that I love you and miss you so much... You must know, you're not alone. I'm here... And we'll fight for you to get out of that place...*

I can hardly get beyond the first line. There are suddenly hot tears scalding my eyes, blurring my vision. And I'm wiping them away furiously so I can read the next line, but they won't stop. They're streaming out of my eyes, misting them over, forcing me to the point where I feel a storm building in the depths of my chest. A swell of emotion is suddenly surging out of my eyes, my throat, my heart. I howl, I sob so hard, so loudly, that the Thai officer standing next to me wants to know what's in this letter.

How do I explain, as a grown woman, that I've been floored by these few simple words? That I'm bawling like a baby because Christine, on the furthest tip of Africa, thousands of kilometres away, loves and misses me? Christine with her loud voice and raucous laughter that vibrates through her short, plump body. This thought pulls me back to school, to the time of ponytails and lunch swaps and shrinking hems.

We start out alone, but gradually find each other – a gang of four inseparable girls who share everything but the same parents. Siamese friends joined at the soul. Barely a day passes when Collette, Christine, Melanie and I do not see or speak to one another.

In that classroom in Eldorado Park, Colette and I are "neighbours", sharing a double-desk. I'm eleven years old and in the middle of a big transition in my life. I've just left my home in Port Elizabeth to move in with my aunt, Rushda, her husband Moegsiem and my cousins, Camilla and Shafiek. I love them, but I've left my mother and sisters behind and Eldorado Park is boisterous and bewildering. I don't understand the ways of people here. Everything they own is bigger and flashier than in the city I come from.

I'm thrust into Grade 6 at McBain Charles Primary School in Johannesburg where everyone seems to be learning at breakneck speed. Collette is the bright spark sitting next to me, and the first girl to offer me her friendship. She's twelve and a serious-faced, no-nonsense type. She always wears her hair neatly tied up and strikes me as having a strong character for a twelve-year-old. Slightly stocky, she wrinkles her face and her eyes disappear when she smiles. There is something trustworthy about this face. Collette is highly intelligent and willing to help me when I struggle with some of our school work. We spend hours doing our homework together and she constantly builds up my self-confidence.

We visit each other's homes often. They're a religious family that goes to church often. She invites me to join the Youth Group and we get involved in many church activities together. Collette and I grow together. We get closer over the years and as I move to a place of greater awareness, I begin to appreciate the joy of being in the presence of someone who doesn't care about the material things but values people above all and wants to live life in all its simplicity. I'm happy to share the difficulties of my life with her, without fear of being judged. She inspires me with her words, and over the years they somehow play a role in shaping me.

Shortly after Collette and I become friends, we get to know Christine, who's also in our class. There's something magnetic about Christine. She's the closest thing to a comedian you'll find at school. But she's also this firebrand, bold and outspoken, who won't hesitate to put you in your place if she feels you've crossed the line. For some reason, she's very protective over me. Maybe, in her eyes, I'm the underdog that she wants to see have its day.

I only get to know Melanie in high school. She's a friend of Christine's from a previous school. My immediate impression is that she's a rowdy creature, who hardly ever gives that high-pitched voice of hers a rest. She speaks in such an animated way sometimes that her big eyes shine and almost double in size when she's telling a story. We tease her about her skinny legs. But she laughs at herself too. Yet there are times when you do glimpse the more serious side of her. She's caring and nurturing. Melanie and Christine are the first to be there whenever you're in trouble. There's a flame inside Melanie, igniting light and laughter in everyone whose life she touches. At my darkest times, she tends the flame in me and never lets it go out.

Melanie lives with her mother, her stepfather and sisters in a big house in Klipspruit. Our families are all very strict, so we make up a list of excuses that we use to get out of the house. Either it's homework or group projects or we have to visit a sick member of the gang! But once we've made our escape, Melanie raids her step-dad's liquor cabinet and we head straight for Collette's sister's house to quench our thirst. After the first round we're giggling, teasing, lightly gossiping. By the end of the afternoon, we cackle loudly, sing horribly out of tune and cry like kids. I'm surprised Collette's sister doesn't throw us out!

In spite of our bad behaviour sometimes and the odd punishment, we stick together. We make excuses for one another. We protect one another. We have our spats, but they don't last long. We talk our problems through in the safety of this cocoon we've created together. They're a soft place to fall, my friends. And that's why I have no secrets from them. All the things I promised myself I would never talk about, I share with them. There comes a day when I realise we've finally grown up, all of us. Moulted out of our childish ways into full-grown women. And after all these years together, I may be closer to them than some of my own blood relatives.

They're thrilled when I hear that I'm a Miss South Africa semi-finalist. I have to re-read it to believe it's true. I'm immediately on the phone to the girls. They're overjoyed for me! The others are tied up at university, but I take Christine and my cousin, Moufida, shopping with me to find the perfect outfits for the next round. I'll have to model a casual outfit, an evening gown and swimwear in front of a panel at the Carlton Centre.

Christine, Moufida and I spend hours trawling the malls, with little success. But Christine won't allow us to give up. She's convinced perfection is just around the corner.

It's quite easy to find casual wear. I walk out with an elegant black-and-white pencil-skirt suit that I feel could be a winner. But the ideal evening gown escapes us for hours, until Oreb Boutique rises up before us like an oasis in a desert of drabness. And there, dangling on a hook, is the white fishtail skirt and top that seduces us all. I love the shape and design. Christine and Moufida say it was made for my figure. The soft wire worked into the sleeves and the hem of the dress create a full effect.

The swimsuit also meets with their approval. I hear Christine's voice now – taking honesty to the extreme, telling me in the crudest terms if I can carry off an outfit or not! When she doesn't like the look, she just laughs at me. What I would give to hear that laughter again! No one in Lard Yao laughs like that. Here, it's as though every smile is laced with an underlying sadness that stains everything. There are too few reasons to laugh in here. Occasionally, the laughter of a prison child seeps through into the gloom of our lives. But we won't let ourselves get used to it. These children only laugh because they don't understand the world they've been born into – a world of bright see-saws, rainbow jungle gyms, gleaming shackles, and women with cloths, wiping blood off the courtyard walls.

At Lard Yao, I'm not sure Christine would laugh either. She'd probably cry if she saw how I came undone over her letter, even though it's planted just the kernel of hope I needed. She wouldn't laugh if she saw how I live here, or how humiliated I am, wearing this uniform every day that marks me as a criminal. Part of me is desperate to see her again, to share this story of what's happened to me in all its grimy detail. But another part of me knows I'd be ashamed if she saw me here, reduced to an animal who shoves at others for my share of food and shits in a hole without walls around it. A girl who once wore an evening dress that turned the judges' heads but can now hardly be asked to clean her face or comb her hair.

The Thai officer who handed me this precious note won't move from the spot until I've translated this letter into English for her. These are the rules, but she also wants to understand what's upset me so much. And when I translate it, she's confused, mystified at how harmless those words are.

I can't explain it either. The secret isn't only in the words I read aloud. It's in the silence in-between. In the unspoken history of so many years of shared hardship that I must now survive on my own. In the sum of hundreds of days of unbroken love and generosity in the lives of three other girls and me. Our extraordinary life lessons of joy, love, hurt, loss and loyalty – the kind that blurs the lines between the people you call your family and those you call your friends. And when this Thai officer sees me sitting there for hours, bent over that one flimsy scrap of paper, soaking up each word like some holy man committing the scriptures to heart, maybe she has some inkling of what I've left behind. I may cry, but somewhere, I am overjoyed. I'm loved. I'm missed. I am remembered.

CHAPTER 8

Felix

Five days after I arrive, arrangements are made for me to move to the mother's room, Poisy. Elise is there too. It's a cell for pregnant women, mothers and infants. Forty women and their children, from newborns to toddlers, share a small, cramped space, eight-by-six metres. The idleness in Poisy is exhausting. We sit in here all day doing almost nothing at all. Each pregnant woman or mother and child is squashed into a small rectangle marked by their towels. Those standing or trying to move around to pacify their screaming babies are mashed in a human press of sweat-drenched bodies. Night never intrudes on us, with the bulbs blazing like floodlights twenty-four hours a day.

I wonder why these newborns who push out of the darkness of their mother's wombs into the blinding lights of Lard Yao are so hasty to come into the world. They cry listlessly for hours, day and night. They never sleep for long. Their mothers' eyes hang, bloodshot and droopy, the strains of their drowsy lullabies lost in the din of constant chatter.

As for the pregnant women, the wardens suddenly treat us like bone china that will shatter if we're not placed out of everyone's reach. This must be part of our punishment for choosing such a rotten introduction to the world for our babies. We spend entire days glued to the same spot, eating, sleeping, swatting insistent mosquitos away from the minute puddles of sweat that pool on our skin. We recycle our conversation, tell the same stories, show the same photos, chew over the same words until there's no taste in them anymore.

But at least there are times of the day when we can leave this hellhole. As soon as the key clicks in the lock of the cell door, I burst out into the blazing sunshine. It stings my skin. But the place I'm going to will be worth it. More and more often these days, I go there to remember who I was before I came here. It sits there empty, waiting for me. A small two-seater bench outside the hospital building that I almost feel I own these days. It overlooks the dam. This is the most peaceful spot in Lard Yao. A slice of heaven in hell. And as I sit down, my mind whispers to my body that not all of me needs to stay here. That if I want, part of me can scale those high, sky-blue walls, and live in another place and time where I'm loved and cared for.

So that's what I've been doing lately. Sitting here like an empty shell of muscle and bone, while my spirit rises up out of me and travels across land, across oceans, across time to my country where my mother, my sisters, Melissa and Jacky, and my precious Aunt Rushda wait for news of what's happened to me. I close my eyes and I'm in Aunty Rushda's house in Eldorado Park. It's small and the phones ring constantly and the visitors stream in. They all want to know where I've gone. Why I left and never came back. But these women and girls I love so much have no answers. They wring their hands and sit there speechless, because they know there's almost nothing that could keep me from them.

My mother and Aunty Rushda look so small, so old. Was that really how they were when I left, or has my disappearance aged them so much in such a short time? My sister, Melissa, is leaning heavily on one elbow, poring over her books, studying for some exam. But she sees nothing on the page. And there is Jacky, my big sister. So mentally fragile. I want to take her in my arms. She sits apart from the others, her thoughts tangled, because she can't understand what's become of me.

And when I can't stand it any longer, I go where my heart

pulls me. To the man I love and long for every day. It's funny how strangely I feel towards him these days. I still love him so much but I'm so angry with him. Why's it taking him so long to find me? In some breaths, I curse him. In others, I speak my undying love to him. In my mind's eye, I can see him banging on doors, begging for information on where I am. But one door after another is slammed in his face and he grows more tired with each one, weary of asking and pleading and being told nothing. He's sitting on the couch in his flat, head in his hands, wondering if he somehow imagined me. Is it possible that this flesh and blood woman, who lay in his bed and ate meals with him and fell pregnant with his child, has suddenly melted and dripped out of existence? It's impossible! The thought's crazy! So his door is flung open again and his feet hit the pavement, scouring the streets to find some trace of me.

And while I tick-tock between love and anger, I feel guilty for expecting so much of him. If I were thinking clearly, I'd understand that he hasn't come to me because he can't. How could he know where I am? Maybe he's being kept from me. It's possible the Thai officials have lied about my whereabouts. I haven't even had a visit from the South African embassy in Bangkok yet. There's no way he knows where I am.

Besides, Felix is the male swan who mates for life. He discovers he loves me when I am seventeen years old – a school girl with two plaits and a broken heart who's shut the door on love after my first relationship ended badly. He's working in the clothing business. And I meet Felix when the company he's working for approaches my agency, looking for models to use in fashion shows. Felix styles me. He has a great eye for what suits my body. He's a model too, an exceptionally good-looking guy, and we end up spending more time together, although only as friends.

But in time, Felix finds his way into my heart. He tries, hard as he can, to heal the hole in me, to plaster over the cracks with his own friendship – simple, undemanding. It takes us to the tops of hills where we laugh when we see people, small as ants, going about their lives below. We dangle our feet in a stream and eat cheese sandwiches and talk for hours, and I suddenly know this is a man I can be foolish with. So I don't feel bad about the times he's held me, while I bawled from heartache, till my eyes were two swollen red mounds. I don't care that this man, who first saw me at my best on the catwalk, sees me barefoot, without a smudge of make-up, in my oldest tracksuit pants. I only care that he's fallen in love with me the way I have with him. And on the hilltop that day, I make a silent wish that for the rest of my life and his, my eyes will fall upon his face every day.

Of all the things I could've wished for. Of all the things I wish for still today. Felix would love me, right here in my drab prison uniform with my knotty, unkempt hair. He'd sit beside me on this bench telling me how achingly beautiful I am to him, even though I know this prison does nothing to keep me looking healthy. I wish, above all, just to see his face. To fix my eyes on it again – his subtle features, his skin like dark velvet. I close my eyes and caress it. I know its every line, its every contour. And now that I'm here and I can't touch his face anymore, I find myself yearning to see it more than I ever have. If I stay locked up here for years, how will the landscape of this face change when I'm gone? And who will step in to touch it in my absence?

At this moment, this loneliness I feel is an industrial-size vacuum cleaner plugged into me, sucking out every drop of blood, every organ, every nerve, every sinew, every fibre, every cell, all gushing backwards through its pipe, leaving just a dry, crusty, hollow husk of me behind. I crave him. He's a drug I would smoke, swallow, sniff, shoot up my veins, overdose on. A drag of Felix. Just one last hit of him! To grip his face between my hands as he takes me to his bed, plants his mouth on mine and tells me no one will ever take me from him. To feel his hands reaching up along my body, his dark form, suspended over mine. The first time I press my body against his, the taste of him in my mouth is so familiar, so safe. Somewhere, I'm telling myself to be careful, to cling to self-control. But the bonds that hold me shatter and we fall into a slow caress, fluid, as though our bodies have known each other before this. In the tenderness of his touch, my shame flees and my body gives way to his. Our shadows are stretched large, elastic, across the walls. We merge – Felix and I – into one body. The miracle inside me is ignited. I lie in the dark, my virginity spent, listening to him breathe.

Six weeks later, we're walking out of a shop, hand in hand, in the middle of Jo'burg when I feel my legs go limp and I almost collapse in the street. Felix breaks my fall. I open my eyes minutes later in the doctor's surgery. And he's standing over me, stethoscope around his neck, a pregnancy test in hand. It's positive. I don't know how to react. I've just heard I'm in the Miss South Africa semi-finals. I also want to make a go of Vinni Montana, the clothing business Felix and I have started together at the Carlton Centre. I have plans to study so I can be a social worker one day. I'll have to learn to balance all these responsibilities with motherhood. Felix sees no obstacles, though. He's so overjoyed, he could kiss the doctor.

A few nights later, he takes me out to dinner at an expensive restaurant. And I when my back is turned, there's a small splash in my wine glass. Three diamonds encrusted in an elegant ring. Lying at the bottom of my glass like sunken treasure. I trawl in there to fish it out. It comes out glinting. I love it. It's beautiful. I'm just not quite ready yet. He's slightly hurt. But he's never one to give up. "We have to give this child a name, a home, a family. It's the right thing to do, Vinni." I always want to do the right thing. I put the ring on. Ask him to make me a stupid promise that he'll tell no one we're engaged yet. The ring fits nicely, but I can't keep it on all the time. Some days, it feels like a diamond noose. But every day he watches me with it. If I take it off, he reminds me to put it back on. One day, when I leave it at Aunty Rushda's place after washing dishes there, he rushes over to get it back.

But I overlook it when he's pushy sometimes. He's a man who knows what he wants and I can't punish him for that. We've already been in business for a year. We have our own West African tailor who's a wizard with the needle. We're turning a profit and he feels it's time to expand. He decides I have to go to Thailand to scout some new fashion for the store. I'll look for samples, source some well-priced suppliers and take pictures of some of the latest fashions to use in our designs. We can't just shut the business down to go off on a shopping trip together. So he'll keep the shop running while I'm away.

Now, as I sit here, watching the stillness of the sky reflected on the dam's surface, I can't help wondering what would've happened if Felix had come with me. Maybe he would've noticed something suspicious about the books and tossed them out. Or maybe he would've offered to put the books in his bag, in which case I'd be fighting the Thai justice system to free the man I love.

But today, I'm hopeful that this moment, on this bench overlooking the dam, could somehow be magical. I once heard someone say that love is the most elastic of human emotions. It stretches across time, across countries, across oceans. And if that's true, then Felix is sitting somewhere halfway across the world, feeling just like me. Maybe he's even hearing the words of my heart across the distance. So I close my eyes and speak to him, whispering his name under my breath. *Come Felix. Save me from this bitter place. I've never needed your love more than I do right now.*

When I get up to walk away, I suddenly feel a charge enter my body. And in that moment, I'm convinced he's heard me.

CHAPTER 9

Friends

I am a prisoner in this hellhole, but I must pay for it!

Nothing at this prison is free. Everything needed here – prison uniforms, bags, food, water and toiletries – must be bought. For a while, I have no money and the other prisoners give me their hand-me-downs. But I soon put the money left over from my travels into my prison account so I can buy what I need. It's possible for people from outside to send us parcels of food, clothing and toiletries, but there's no guarantee that we'll get them. We're often at the mercy of the guard on duty.

Because of the political change in South Africa, the exchange rate between the baht and the rand in 1994 ranges between five and eleven rand to one baht, which makes things expensive for me. But there's a coupon system in prison, so we never handle cash. Each coupon has an expiry date on it, so if you don't use it, you lose the money. We can request a maximum of 100 baht from our prison accounts daily to cover our expenses, although that amount is only paid out weekly. The wardens give us a slip of paper, containing our names and prison numbers. We list the amount of money we want to withdraw from our bank books. They hand out our coupons every morning, just before we leave our cells.

The first things I buy are toilet paper and toothpaste. Once a week, I pay a girl 10 baht to queue in a choking line for my water. I share some water with her. While she queues, I head for the bakery and buy half a loaf of bread. I have some of it with tea for breakfast. But often, I can't afford to buy food from the *lanka* and I'm forced to eat at the dining hall, the *gong li un* where government food is served. We queue in the scalding sun and are fed in relays. Sometimes, the queues are so long that by the time we get to the front, the food is finished. We always keep a close eye on what we're eating here. Before the food is taken into the hall, it's left out in the open, so it's often contaminated by insects or birds outside. There are also worms in the vegetables. And I've found writhing maggots in the red rice, but I just picked them out and ate the rice because I was starving and there was no money to buy food. The food improves slightly when a new prison director takes over. But when I can afford it, I still buy a watery gravy called *gang* with rice. It's served in plastic bags. Sometimes, I mix tuna with rice and at other times, I spoil myself with a bit of fruit.

Very few prisoners can afford to buy food luxuries like sugar or sandwiches. That's why there's so much theft at Lard Yao. Even those who are sent parcels from their families don't always receive them. Some wardens hold onto the items, like toiletries or beauty products, and make prisoners pay a "rental" fee each time they want to use them.

Lard Yao is a stand-alone world. A place like Earth, except the people who live in it live by a system that makes them stand apart from the human race. Many of us have a vague memory of being human, but as time goes, it fades. Some of us long to return to it. But while we're here, we can never forget that either what we've done, or what we've been accused of doing, means we can never walk among ordinary people again until we've paid our dues.

There are days when I feel I'd rather go before a firing squad than live in this place where the air flows hot, like lava, into my lungs and the sun wages its own scorching war on me from the outside. When it rains, the prison is waterlogged. There's hardly any shelter from the downpour because the rain gushes through the bars. So we wade from one building to another and eat our mushy rained-on meals, standing almost knee-deep in water. The place is overrun by rats. Large and bloated, grown chunky from the few small scraps in our bags, they roam the grounds, furry hunters, brazen and thieving. Glaring at those who challenge them. They eat our bags, our soap, our shoes, our toothpaste, our mats, our food.

Only the feral cats keep the rats in check. Warders catch the felines and throw them out. But they soon make their way back, their kittens suddenly appearing in dark corners, their laser eyes trained on you.

There are strips of flowers planted outside the offices and along a path where visitors enter. They contrast with the buildings where we're forced to work, bathe, eat and sleep every day. These structures are so old and run down that some of them are almost falling to pieces. Even in the newer buildings, the lacquer peels like scabs from wounds that won't heal. It would be the easiest thing to slap on a coat of paint every now and then, just to make our surroundings look a little more cheerful. But our captors won't have us sit in these gardens all day, pumped up full of pleasant thoughts. Jail is meant to be suffering.

Lard Yao is never just full. It's always overflowing. There are five thousand of us in its walls, but there's always place for one more in the swollen belly of this beast that needs constant feeding. I'm one of more than a hundred and seventy foreign nationals, not counting the other Asians like Cambodians, Chinese, Koreans and Vietnamese. There's a group of South Africans here. Many of them were arrested at around the same time as me. But it's really the other foreigners I've become close to.

An American woman named Virginia and I are the only two foreigners in the hospital. Virginia isn't pregnant, she's just ill. But we're both so relieved to have another English speaker to talk to that we fall into easy conversation, sharing intimate details of our lives. She has young daughters who are now being raised by her family. Her stories mostly centre on her life in the hoods of New York City and how gangsterism drew her like voodoo into street fights and gun violence. I'm highly amused by her impersonations of the gang members she used to hang out with. "You think you're so fly with your big ass!" she says, sashaying around. "I'll show you!" She makes me laugh hard.

I befriend another American who couldn't be more different to Virginia. Olivia Reece is a golden-haired foul-mouthed Rasta from California, who loves Snoop Dogg and smokes marijuana. She revels in dancing barefoot, tossing her blonde mane as her body pulsates to the music. She's married to a Nigerian serving time in Klong Prem. Her two-year-old daughter, Tiffany, streams into my life like pure liquid sunshine. Tiffany has a sibling on the way, so I do my best to help take care of her to take the pressure off Olivia. As happy as being with Tiffany makes me, sometimes when we're outside and she's kicking her legs high up into the air on that swing, giggling shyly as falling snowflakes, something grabs my heart and squeezes it so violently, I can hardly breathe. That's when I see my child where Tiffany now sits, playing, having the most fun prison-children can within these walls. I love my unborn child enough to know this isn't a place to grow up. I must find a way for my baby to be free.

Yet another American girl who visits the hospital quite by chance ends up as one of my best friends in prison. La Tasha Madson is a year younger than me, a well-toned hip-hop dancer from Los Angeles with a small build and short dreadlocks. They frame her beautiful, chocolate face. The story of how she came here is similar to many I've heard. Girl meets boy. Girl falls for boy. Boy asks girl to carry a bag for him. Girl earns a lifetime behind bars. She admits it must've been easy to trap her. For all her good looks, her ability to paint and dance so well, she has a low self-esteem. It must have something to do with her having left home when she was very young.

Then there's Mildred Atta, a self-confessed Ghanaian mafia queen. If anyone had told me I'd one day have a drug kingpin for a friend, I'd have laughed at them. She tells me police long suspected she was running a syndicate. But they only manage to convict her by planting some drugs in her hotel room. She admits to being in charge, but swears she never had any drugs in her possession.

54

When she comes to Lard Yao, she leaves her three young sons behind. Their uncle is cruel to them and neglects them. But the boys struggle on for many years to try to overcome their circumstances.

Another close friend, Kairit Aron, is from Estonia. She comes to Lard Yao not being able to speak any English at all. But she approaches me, one day, asking me to teach her English. I make her read the Psalms from the Bible and write letters to me for practice. It annoys her that she has to read the Bible every day, but her English gradually improves. She's also been arrested for drug trafficking but she claims she never agreed to carry drugs for anyone – although she did agree to smuggle diamonds. Over the years, Kairit proves to be a person who gives me the gift of her honesty when everyone else is watering down the truth.

These are the friends who become my family in the absence of my flesh-and-blood relatives. We eat, sleep, work, laugh and cry with one another. Together we restore our hope, awaken new worlds within us. Make ourselves believe that as difficult as things are, we can brave it as a human chain and come out alive on the other side.

My friends also begin to nudge me towards an understanding that, in the short time ahead, I'll have to learn the delicate art of balance if we – my child and I – are going to survive this. I must never lose my will to leave here or stop fighting to prove my innocence, but every moment we are forced to be here, I must make sure that our existence is bearable.

Now I understand why some women in here braid their hair and put on make-up. They won't let themselves waste away until the day their freedom comes. From the moment I realise this, I begin to do it too. I clean myself up and look presentable. I allow my friends to sit with me like mentors and teach me everything they can about this world of Lard Yao.

I learn not to step on the Thai women's blue hessian mats that they call "home" and consider sacred. I never show the bottom of my foot because it offends them. I turn a blind eye to their coughing in my face or plucking their underarms with tweezers, in full view of everyone. And as much as I detest them, I even make peace with the fact that rats, lizards, snakes, flying cockroaches and hundreds of feral cats are part of the Lard Yao experience.

I take ownership of two lockers and, two weeks later, buy myself a bag from the *lanka*. And when I see it sitting there in the corner, among the pile of bags, some newer, others worn ragged with time, I begin to accept that no matter how hard I've tried to deny it, I am one of these women now. A Lard Yao inmate like all the rest.

The cracks in the old wooden floor are so large I can see down to the room below. I keep staring down there, trying to burn that image into my memory because it reminds me of what will happen if I don't take control. My child and I will simply fall through the cracks like dust off old shoes. I can't let it happen. I'll fight with every last grain of my being for this baby. Even if I have to shout it out to every visitor who walks through these prison gates, I'll make sure we are never forgotten.

CHAPTER 10

Unexpected visitor

In the weeks that follow, the South African embassy sends Mr Koch, a distinguished man, well dressed, reserved and formal, to meet me. I'm so excited the first time I see him, I almost cry with happiness! It feels like Mr Koch's come to rescue me from hell – a neutral eye over this prison, ensuring I'm in good health and not being ill treated.

But the other women warn me against expecting miracles. Mr Koch is no saviour on a white horse sweeping in here to carry me out. He's a foreign diplomat, who has to respect the laws of the country he's working in. One morning, Mr Koch tells me the South African embassy in Pretoria has told my family where I'm being held. This news is a blast of Arctic air in this boiling, dank embassy room with its rickety benches and mangled wire gauze. Now that Felix knows, he will come. I literally tear out of that room to tell all my friends the news. Felix knows – and he's coming! I can feel it!

I live in new hope after that. Life in Lard Yao remains hard, but I teach myself to smile again. Sometimes I even laugh, and my friends are happy to see the change in me. The news elevates me closer to the sun, which can now shine into the blackness of this hovel that's become my life in recent weeks. May comes, loiters and drifts off, every day holding the promise of this meeting and stealing it away from me as the sun goes down. But I won't allow myself to be discouraged. I imagine my reunion with Felix. He won't be able to hold me or touch me, which is what I've longed for. But at least he'll be there in the flesh, sitting opposite me, reassuring me, delighting in the little bump bulging from my stomach as my pregnancy nears 4½ months.

But the days continue to pass, reckless and dizzying, stepping over each other to ring in the next sunrise, the next sunset. And there's suddenly an unease bubbling inside me. I pray for patience, because that is what's so easily lost in a timeless place like Lard Yao, where each day becomes a fusion of the next, until weeks and months and even years have disappeared beneath your feet. But time begins to wrinkle and I can feel my hope wilting.

Now my friends rarely mention Felix's name. They don't want to disappoint me further. The other inmates are spoilt with visits from relatives who are mortgaging their homes to send their jailed loved ones money, or buying expensive tickets to Thailand on the off-chance they'll get to spend just half an hour in the presence of these women they love so much. My mother and sisters can't afford it, but Felix could. He could write me a letter if he cared enough.

One morning in early June, I'm called to a meeting with a Mr Naidoo, an embassy official who's apparently visiting the group of South Africans behind bars. But I get there late and I'm just about to rush into the embassy room, when one of the wardens asks, "*Paai-jeem-mai?*" (Are you going to visit?) I tell her I will, although I'm not quite sure who this official is. "It is Mr Naidoo." She thrusts his passport, with its small black photo, under my nose, and there, like a punch in the chest, Felix is staring back at me.

Oh my God! He came! My hands are shaking. He's finally come to take me back home with him! But why the hell is he using a false passport? If they find out, they'll lock him up! I have to take a moment to slow my breathing. Stop my heart from pounding against my ribs like it'll shatter them. I don't know what to say to him. And then, I'm smoothing my hair, my clothes. What will he think when he sees me in this awful prison uniform?

I take one purposeful step closer and peer into the room. I can see the outline of him there. I enter slowly, look up, and see the bench lined with a queue of women, some of them my friends, all with their backs to me. I stand and watch and listen. I hear their laughter. I watch the way they toss their heads and tease and chatter and smile. And I see how he casts his spell over them. His words, his charm, his face. My Felix. My hypnotic Felix. He's a god basking in his own worship, craving more; angling his body flirtatiously, throwing them scraps of his attention, reeling them in like a shoal of desperate fish. It sickens me.

The rage is gathering inside me like a swarm of wasps. But I have to keep my emotions in check. If I don't, I'll be hauled out of here and thrown into solitary confinement. I sit down on the bench quietly. Felix notices me squeezing in but we can't see each other very well from where I'm sitting. All I can make out is that he's lost weight since the last time I saw him. I want to get closer. I know Felix's emotions live in his eyes. And as I shuffle nearer and look directly into them, I can see him fighting to control that emotion just so he stays composed in the presence of the other women. The others leave. And the room recedes. And we're locked there, Felix and me, searching each other's eyes.

This is not how I imagined it would be. But the first thing I ask him is, "How do you know the rest of the South Africans?"

"The embassy made a mistake", he says. "They were only supposed to call you out."

"But why've you come on a false passport, Felix?"

"It would've taken too long to get my papers together. I risked my life coming here to see you, Vinni. I needed to see you and find out how I could get you out of this place…"

"Where's Jackson? Have you seen him?"

"No," he says. "He's just disappeared. No one can find him."

This upsets me so much. How can it be that Jackson is walking free while I've been shut up in here for three monstrous months with such little hope of getting out? I start to cry. All I want is the truth. Felix doesn't know the horror of the nights I've had to lie on the floors of these filthy jail cells, weeping for him, crying out his name, begging for him to come and get me. I look at this man I love so much and I'm filled with doubt. I don't know what to believe anymore.

"Felix, I am fucking hurting," I say through my tears. "I'm sitting behind bars and I can't stand this. I need you to get me out of here. Take me home! Please."

"I gave your picture to *You* magazine," he says. "We need help to get you out. I love you Vanessa. This is not easy for me."

And when he returns the next day, there's no more hope than there was the day before. He's confused about the laws of Thailand and still doesn't know how he can help me. He says he's tried to get me a lawyer but this man is demanding a lot of money, which he doesn't have.

"When I go back home, I'll go and see your family and we'll try to raise the money for a lawyer, Vinni," he promises me.

While Felix is in Thailand, I'm taken to the magistrate's court for another appearance. He comes to the court and as I get out of the back of that van, I'm so humiliated that he should see me chained this way. It affects him deeply. Desperate, Felix asks the court lawyer representing me if there's anything he can do to help me. The answer is no. There's no ruling in my case that morning. But as I leave the building, Felix and I grab hold of each other and he kisses me. Feeling him close to me after all that's happened is reassuring and overwhelming. But I'm so emotional, so frustrated, that I start arguing with him. He tries to make me see it from his point of view. "Vanessa, I'm trying. I'll try my best to get this money together and hire a decent lawyer for you."

But that's not enough. I need the truth, right now.

"Felix. Look at me – I'm carrying your baby and I'm in prison! I don't have money, or support, or anything that I need for the baby. All I want to know is, did you know about the drugs?"

He shakes his head in disbelief.

"Vanessa I would never risk our baby's life or yours." He looks hurt for a moment. "I never used drugs. You know that. Jackson used me too. He used both of us."

During what remains of our visiting time at Lard Yao, we talk in circles, and rehash what needs to be done to get me out of this place. And when Felix goes, he gives me some money and leaves some baby clothes for me, which I never receive. I'm hoping, praying, that he'll find the money for my legal fees. But not long after his visit, Felix writes to me. He tells me there's no money to pay a lawyer. And I find out he never went to see my family when he returned to South Africa. He communicates less. He sends no more money to support me. I don't understand his silence. I'm angry with him. I write him terrible letters in which I tell him the other women here receive support from the men who love them. I ask him why he won't provide for me and his baby. He writes me a couple of letters back, but I'm so angry, I can't even look at them. Then he stops writing altogether.

A few weeks later, I receive a letter from a complete stranger. She tells me she's pregnant with Felix's child and they're living together. *"Look for another father for your baby when you come home. Felix says he doesn't know how you ended up there and he doesn't know anything about drugs. Felix has sold all your stuff in the apartment and we've bought new things."* I'm shocked. She must've scratched through his papers and found the prison address. I don't respond, but that's how I find out I'm on my own.

A real bitterness towards Felix begins to fester in me. It drips from me, leaving an ugly, acidic trail wherever I walk. I'm summoned back to court. And I wonder if the judge sees a change in me. If he wonders who planted this wildness, this rage in my eye. There's still no ruling because the police don't show up. But I suddenly realise my passport is gone. The police must've confiscated it during my interrogation at the airport. It's another worrying sign that I'm not getting out of Thailand anytime soon.

I have no money. The last bit from my travels has run out. My child will be born in a matter of 4½ months, and how will I meet my newborn's needs with the little I have? If my baby cries from starvation, it will break my heart, but I will have nothing to give. In July, I nervously pen a letter to Nelson Mandela, South Africa's first democratic president. I congratulate him on his election victory and his inauguration that I know will set South

Africa on the path to peace. And then, I tell him my story. Maybe someone who's spent his entire youth behind bars will understand how much I fear the same happening to me. The letter is published in the *Sunday Times*:

"I am so confused, I don't know what to do. On 25 July I am going to court again where I will have to plead guilty to avoid receiving the death sentence or life in prison. We don't get any medical help and we sleep on the floor with one towel, in a small room that we share with 60 other women. Each of us sleeps on two rows of tiles. We have to buy everything in here, even the prison uniforms and it can be very hard trying to survive in here... Please, I beg you to help us to escape from this planet... I hope and pray that you will help us and think about my child's future..."

I don't hear from him and I'm not surprised. He has too many pressing issues to take care of as South Africa's new leader. What's Felix's excuse? The least he can do is cater for his child. But he won't. I know Felix. This baby and I are the stone around his neck dragging him down into the depths below, while he longs to breathe the air at the surface. A twin source of shame, because he's not capable of the kind of love it takes to look after your fiancée and your child when they're behind bars.

I'm broken by what Felix has done to me. Nothing has ever hurt as much as his betrayal. I suppose I never really understood love. I only thought I did. And I know I can't tear myself away from Felix slowly. The longer it takes, the more it will hurt. All I want is one slash – deep, quick, bloodless. A steel blade raised above my heart. A shortcut to the hurt. It flashes. I plunge it in deep. Force it downwards. Gasp from the vertical stab of pain that slices so neat, so spotless through this vein of love, memory, heartache that was once Felix and me. But he's gone. He slips, unseen, like a wisp of muslin from my soul. There is no more Felix and me. Only us two. My child and me.

CHAPTER 11

Bond

He arrives unexpectedly at the prison one morning towards the end of July, three months after my arrest. A pitbull in an avocado suit, stark against the beigeness of Lard Yao. At first, I'm nervous about this stranger who arrives from South Africa out of the blue, claiming to want to help me. He sits opposite me in the embassy room. Introduces himself as Mpumelelo "Bond" Nyoka. Says I can call him Bond. There's something flamboyant about him with his curved moustache and longish, straightened hair that he combs backwards. His glasses give him a look of seriousness and intelligence. He says he's a lawyer.

He must think I'm an idiot. It's obvious Jackson or Obey, maybe even Felix, sent him to check up on me. But Bond says he doesn't know them. He's come to Thailand because he read about me in the newspapers and my story really touched him. A lawyer? Touched by my story? Back home, they're known as sharks. They'll fight for people and when they win, disappear with most of the settlement. I'm finding Bond's story a little hard to swallow.

He presents me with a full list of his credentials. They look convincing on paper. If all of this is true, he's a successful, highly qualified lawyer. He talks to me about some of the cases he's fought in the past and his successful outcomes. I'm beginning to believe him. Then he says he went to see my mother and my Aunt Rushda before leaving for Bangkok, to tell them he was coming to visit me. He reassures me that all's well at home and despite the news of my arrest, my family members are trying to do their best to continue with their lives, although they're constantly anxious about me. He gives me some small gifts from my aunt that she knew I wanted: toiletries, underwear and chocolates. Now I believe him.

That day, Bond spends three hours with me, talking about the possibility of representing me and fighting my case. I can't believe my luck. There are so many other South Africans in this jail who would kill for a lawyer like Bond. But he's chosen me. I fill him in on everything, from the moment I leave South Africa to the discovery of the drugs at Don Muang Airport, to what life is like for me in Lard Yao. He listens. He takes notes. He asks detailed questions. He seems to have a rock-hard determination. It sets his eyes alight when he talks about his legal strategy. Bond has several ideas on how my case could be fought. He knows South African law well but he's also familiarised himself with Thailand's laws.

He explains to me that countries have different ways of dealing with their citizens arrested abroad. Britain and the United States, for example, have prisoner transfer treaties with the Thai government. If their citizens are convicted of a crime in Thailand, they'll serve a small portion of their sentence in this country and then be sent back home where they're usually released after two to three months. In the case of American citizens, if they get a life sentence, they'll spend eight years in a Thai jail and then be transferred home. If it's lower than a life sentence, they'll spend four years behind bars in Thailand and return to their country, usually to be released within a month or two.

The bad news is, South Africa has no such treaty. But it's just a matter of time before one is signed. Nelson Mandela's new government has taken a number of steps towards closing this deal, and Robert McBride of South Africa's Foreign Affairs Department is doing everything in his power to make sure it happens soon. Bond believes this could be my ticket out of Lard Yao. Failing this, he says, we could opt for a pardon from the King of Thailand, but this is an expensive process we should try to avoid unless the extradition treaty falls through.

It's a lot of information for me to absorb all at once and I'm full of questions that he answers patiently and simply. On the one hand, he's formal and clinical. On the other hand, there's a very human side to him. He laughs a lot in-between and lightens my mood too. He tells me he knows my name means "butterflies". So for the remainder of our discussions, he calls me Butterfly. The more we speak, the more I start to trust him.

At the end of that first visit, he asks me if there's anything I need. I'm a little embarrassed to ask for anything. But when he presses me, I ask him for some food, explaining that without money, it's hard to get by in here. He comes back the next day with armfuls of KFC, cakes, cheese and fruit. He's also bought me some towels, socks and Japanese food. The socks are plastered with stars and cartoon characters. "What's this?" I ask him, laughing. "I don't know," he shrugs. "I thought they were nice and you might need them," he chuckles.

Bond stays in Thailand for the remainder of that week. And like clockwork, he's there every day, discussing the finer details of my case for hours. He also brings me food every time he visits – a standard meal of KFC. "Don't they sell any other type of food in Bangkok?" I ask him cheekily. "I don't know what's in the other food," he tells me. "But I know there's chicken in KFC, okay?" This is a standing joke each time he visits. Bond also deposits money into my prison book and at the bakery for me so I can buy food there after he leaves.

On his second visit, I can see Bond's uneasy and slightly less chatty than the first time. "What's wrong?" I ask him and he hesitates slightly. "Vanessa, I don't have good news. It's your mother – she's been involved in a serious car accident…"

And then I suddenly know what he really means, because just a sliver of it flashes through my mind again. This horrible dream I've had for three nights now that my mother is hurt, not because she's been in an accident, but because she's tried to kill herself.

"Bond, tell me the truth – what's wrong with my mother?"

"She was badly injured, but the doctors say she'll recover."

"Was she really in a car crash? I want the truth, Bond. Tell me the truth!"

He breathes out deeply.

"Bond, did my mother try to kill herself?"

"Yes," he says softly. "Yes, she did. Twice."

"*How*? How did she do it? Tell me!"

"She tried to set herself alight. But your sister, Melissa, arrived home right then and she saved her."

"How badly hurt is she? Is she going to make it? Come on, Bond! I need to know!"

"She'll make it, she'll make it. Look, she's going to be in hospital for a long time. Her face isn't burnt at all, but her chest, her breasts, her stomach and one arm were badly burnt. She'll have to have skin grafts... But she just needs time to heal. She'll get there... I'm sorry."

The news shatters me. And for a long time, I blame myself for what's happened to my mother. I'm relieved that she's alive, but after all the hardship she's suffered in her life, I feel I've just gone and made it worse. A relative's just written to me saying no one's even allowed to speak of my imprisonment in my mother's house. I know she's fragile. She's always tried to be strong for us, but underneath her tough skin is a sensitive human being, hurt so easily. I should've known she'd try to do something like this. Not long after this news, I receive a letter from Melissa in which she tells me our sister Jacky is pregnant. I become frantic over how she'll manage to take care of her baby, especially now that my mother's in hospital.

Hearing news like this from a lawyer could be so much more traumatic if that person weren't Bond. But he becomes more than just my lawyer. He becomes my friend. During his stay, he comes to the prison several times. The meetings we have are lengthy. But he doesn't ask for a cent. He talks about his father who was a doctor – a good man who sometimes only charged his patients five rand for a medical examination. "Five rand?" I say. "That can't have been worth his while."

"Well, he taught me it's not all about money, Butterfly. Sometimes it's just about the satisfaction of doing good. You're not only successful by accomplishment."

Bond never visits a single tourist site when he comes to Bangkok and, at the end of our meetings, goes straight back to his hotel room to write up the day's notes on our visit. He even keeps it a secret from his wife that all this work is being done *pro bono*.

I try to impress upon him during our discussions that my innocence is important to me and I want it to form the core of this case. I know I never intentionally committed a crime and it's important to me that Bond knows I'm innocent too. I ask him one day, "You've heard me speak of my innocence so many times. But do you believe me, Bond? Do you believe in your heart that I'm innocent?" And he looks up from the reams of notes he's making and says coolly, "Yes, I do. But that's not the point."

"Of course it is! Why would you want to defend a woman you know is guilty, especially when you're not being paid for it?"

He takes his glasses off and looks me in the eye. "That is not the point. The point is, the punishment doesn't fit the crime. It's disproportionate and that means that if you were convicted of the same crime in our country, you would not get the death penalty, you would not serve a life sentence. The young people in here commit a crime at the most impressionable age of their adult lives and instead of punishing them for a short time, rehabilitating them so they can be reintegrated into society, they are demonised forever. This is a system that says if you make a terrible mistake as a young adult, you must pay for it for the rest of your life! It outrages my sense of justice! And that is why it doesn't matter to me whether you are guilty or not. It matters only that you don't end up paying for it the rest of your life."

Sometimes, Bond's thinking is beyond me. I suppose I'm so wrapped up in my own day-to-day survival that I don't sit down and try to understand all his high-minded reasons. At least I know each time Bond leaves, my case never just sits at the bottom of a pile. He's working on it all the time. Approaching senior South African government officials. Going to their offices in person to plead my case. Talking to the South African media regularly to ensure that my case is still top of mind.

Bond has also found a new following at home. I'm a mixed-race South African, and each time Bond has dealings with the coloured community now, he suddenly finds such acceptance and warmth there. In a country struggling to come to terms with racial integration after apartheid, this is a small miracle that opens doors for Bond and amazes him. In the same way, through my interactions with him, I realise that this fear of black Africans I've had since my arrest makes no sense. I'm reminded that criminals come in all skin-types, as do decent people. And Bond is probably a good example of that.

He never allows himself the luxury of disappointment. Even when his brother receives threatening phone calls warning Bond to stay away from my case, he presses on. He doesn't know who the calls are from but he'd rather focus on my case than wasting time wondering about that. He looks over his shoulder, but he presses on.

I can't imagine what I could've done to attract such a dedicated lawyer. He keeps me updated on news from home. And he tries to uplift me at the times when I'm most discouraged. One day I say to him, "I don't understand why this happened to me. I don't deserve it, do I?"

He pauses for a moment and thinks hard.

"Vanessa, when I look at you, I see a white, Chinese, South American, coloured, black woman. You are yourself, but you're so many people at the same time. And then it makes me think that you stand for all of these women – everyone locked up here, no matter what colour they are, no matter where they come from, no matter how rich or poor they are. You're a symbol of each one of them because when I look at you, I see the suffering of them all, but I also see beyond your identity to your humanity. I have no other explanation for why you came here, except to say that when your story is heard, it'll be the story of every woman who's suffered in Lard Yao. And maybe that will bring some change. But don't worry. Mark my words: whatever you've suffered, whatever's been done to you, you'll be compensated for it forty times over."

And as he packs his bag to go, all I can think is, I hope you're more than just my lawyer, Bond. I hope you're a prophet too.

CHAPTER 12

Body invasion

There's a war going on in my body. I've been taken over by this tiny alien that eats all my meals, throws some up and sends every bit of nutrition to its command centre in the middle of me. That's where this little life has run everything from for the last seven months. It's sent hormones gushing through my system, making me cry and laugh in the same breath. It's drawn the last drop of energy out of me so I can hardly stand some days. And now, it's changing me on the outside, remoulding my frame, each day making it slightly more unfamiliar to me. My taut skin is now magically elastic, my ironing-board tummy punched outwards by this growing mound.

After the first four months are over, so is the worst of my morning sickness. But it's replaced by the most bizarre cravings. I'll eat or drink anything sour I can find. And I often satisfy this with small green Keiffer limes, that I slice in half, coat liberally with salt and eat all the way down to their skins! A tea-drinker all my life, I'm suddenly driven wild by the smell of coffee and begin to drink it black, bitter and in bucketfuls. My friends tell me not to overdo it, because it'll make the baby restless. But I can't help it. And my child spends whole nights jolting me awake with its constant kicking.

These are the small pleasures I live for now – coffee and limes. Bigger dreams have come my way and moved on. I slowly come to accept that Miss South Africa isn't in my future, although it seemed so close to being realised at the time. It's ironic that when I went shopping with Christine and Moufida for my Miss SA outfits, I didn't even know I was pregnant. As a mother, I wouldn't be able to compete anyway.

When I think of it now, the afternoon of the audition for the semi-finals seems so frivolous. I'm thrust into the waiting room, feeling like I've walked into an art gallery displaying three hundred flawless bodies, sculpted to perfection by God himself. I feel like a peasant among beauty queens, curves spilling over their corsets, satin and lace gliding over silken skin. Everything of mine, in comparison, is understated and simple.

But when I sit opposite the judging panel, I give them the best answers I can in the interview. The evening gown section proves to be the easiest for me. But the swimsuit section is more demanding because we model on a table, while the judges view us from an unflattering angle below. And despite the doubt weighing on me for weeks, the letter finally arrives saying I've made it into the semi-finals.

My memories of that time are bittersweet. They remind me that I once had plans for my life. I've long nurtured the dream of becoming a social worker, and modelling would've been a way of paying for my studies. I suppose my family background has shaped me into a person who wants to deaden other people's pain. But right now, I need to think about my own difficulties. It's hard enough living in this jail, but I'll soon have to plan for the survival of two people.

There's this living, breathing, human being taken root inside me. I lie on my back breathing in and out, deep and slow, watching this mysterious mound attached to me rise and fall in such a strange way, it feels like the presence of an alien inside me. I try to make out the shape of a foot or an elbow sticking out, so I'm reassured it's human. And I feel the physical join between us but no emotional one. Other women come to terms with this so easily. Why can't I? All I know is, now that this child of mine has no father, I'm going to have to love this baby enough for both of us.

The lack of proper medical attention at Lard Yao makes my situation worse. There's no proper pre-natal care here. A doctor comes to Lard Yao once a week or we have to either go to King's Hospital, or to the men's prison, Klong Prem, next door for medical attention. Dr One-Eye is frightening. Hunched and aging, his patch is pulled, sinister, over one eye. He's deathly skinny, his flesh pulled over his bones like a badly cut canvas. He studies me, then gropes his way across until he finds my breasts. I'm scheduled for my first check-up with him in August, when I'm almost seven months pregnant. Up to that point, I have had to hope for the best.

Sometimes, Dr Panapong takes over. He's younger, slightly effeminate and skinny with long hair that makes you think he should've been a rock star. He speaks perfect English and he's good-natured. On two occasions I'm also taken to King's Hospital to have scans. But none of them reveals the sex of my child. The trips to the hospital are uncomfortable journeys, hot and exhausting. But at least in the hospital cell at Lard Yao we have a gentle prison inmate who takes care of us.

In the seventh month of my pregnancy, I suddenly take ill. My temperature shoots up, I suffer from constant diarrhoea and vomiting and I'm nauseous all the time. The doctor at the hospital tells me that my body is just struggling to cope with the pressure a baby's put on it. He says it'll continue this way until my child is born.

Because I'm pregnant, I'm not expected to work. But I'll soon be desperate for money to keep my child alive. I find work at the factory where artificial flowers are manufactured for sale outside the prison. It's a typical production line, with each table making one element that will be assembled to create an artificial flower. At my table, we make the flowers' stalks. It's not very mentally stimulating or too strenuous. But the factory's located right at the back of the building and the ventilation is very poor. It makes for a hot, stuffy working environment and there are days when I fall fast asleep at the table. Fortunately, I'm not alone in this factory. Sybil, an older woman, sits next to me. Elise works at a table not far away.

I'm happy to have a job at the flower factory, but I can't work there for much longer. As my pregnancy continues, the heat inside the building becomes overpowering. So I leave to go and work at *chak song*, the factory where they cut threads off garments. This building is a lot cooler and better ventilated because it's close to the prison gates. I also have a chair to sit on, which drastically reduces the number of hours I spend standing.

The hospital occupies one floor of the building I'm now staying in. Elise and I are there together with other women who are on the verge of giving birth. There are only six beds in this room. I sleep on a bed – the first I've been allowed since I came here. Other Thai mothers sleep on the floor.

I can see Elise is feeling the strain of her pregnancy. I sense it won't be long before her baby comes. On the morning it happens, no one reads the signs. Elise eats an apple, and complains of a sore tummy and suddenly, she's in labour. There's no time to take her to a civilian hospital. She'll have to give birth right here at Lard Yao. I'm worried about mother and baby. Without any doctors here, who's going to assist with this birth? Elise is taken downstairs to give birth in the room a floor down. I rush to the window in the hospital room. From here, I can clearly see what's happening below.

Elise is in excruciating pain, her face twisted, her voice being squeezed out through her throat. The officers roughly strap her legs to the table, while she kicks, writhes in pain. I want to shout down to her, that I'm nearby and she'll get through this. But she can't hear me above her own screeching. The more I stare, the more I wonder if that'll be me next.

Elise labours for an hour, which feels more like ten, pushing, resting, gasping, pushing, screaming, pushing. There isn't a single voice to reassure her while she lies there, her legs spread so wide we can all see into her. There is no humanity in this. No respect for the miracle she's about to bring into the world. Elise labours hard. She's exhausted, but she makes one last push to the end. She screams her hardest. Bears down. Propels Baby Jailbird forward with one final push through. Welcome to the world, Adele. Lard Yao has a brand new inmate.

CHAPTER 13

Birth

"Push! Push! Baby about to come!"

I'm strapped to a hospital bed, my back arched, clutching at the sheets, a guttural cry rising from my throat, pushing, thrusting, trying to squeeze this baby out from between my legs. But it's so hard and it hurts so much! I want to scream! I want to claw the walls. I'm begging for painkillers but they won't give me any. Arrrrgggghhh! This small head is a razor inside me, shooting through my cervix like a barbed-wire bullet, tearing flesh, grazing tissue, slicing through me so that the blood comes gushing out.

"Please! I need painkillers..." I'm wailing. *"Please!"* But no one hears me. All these doctors, these nurses standing around and watching me like freak show spectators are shaking their heads. No pills for drug addicts. That's the rule. I want to curse at them – to tell them I'm no drug addict. But who will listen to me now as I lie here, just another piece of prison meat pushing out my young?

Since I went into labour forty-eight hours ago, this baby has tortured me from the inside. Two days of a serrated-edged knife twisting through my kidneys and back. A young mother at Lard Yao hospital shakes her head. "You're having contractions," she says. This motherhood thing is coming. It's upon me. My Rasta-loving, ganja-smoking friend, Olivia, teaches me how to do Lamaze breathing. "Inhale deeply through the nose and exhale through your mouth. You do it like this... Hee hee, hoo hoo!" she says. It does actually help with the pain.

But that pain swells overnight. And nothing can counter it. I throw myself around the bed. I groan. I pant. I cry. The women keep a close eye on how dilated I am. Me (Mother) Lek, our hospital overseer, comes to see me. She rubs my back and my stomach. "Did your water break?" she asks. "I don't know. What does it feel like?" I ask her. "Warm water gushing between your legs." I shake my head. "Wanessa, we can only take you hospital when your water break," she says.

Time trudges from one minute to the next. And the monsoon rains come, hammering like nails into the ground, loud and steady. I wish I could feel those cool drops thrumming on my skin. They'd take this pain away and wash this baby out of me, quick and painless. But the monsoon rains also bring the cold. Hurling myself around on this bed, I begin to feel the heat and cold equally. This throbbing is a fire alight in my stomach, scorching my insides, spreading outwards into my back and thighs, singeing every nerve along the way. But I shiver, as though the rest of me is disconnected from the wildfire in my torso. I cover myself with a blanket, close my eyes and pray for sleep to come.

When light streams through the monsoon clouds, Khun Choem is there. A guard who looks beyond our prison rags to see the human beings underneath. She's here to take me to hospital. I drag myself off the bed, pack some baby clothes and other items, mostly hand-me-downs. Now I must walk to the prison gates a few hundred metres away. Khun Choem supports me while I struggle to stay upright. But there's a flash of nervousness in her eyes. She's desperately hoping I won't give birth on the way to the hospital.

I shuffle along, this massive lump attached to me, almost pushing me over. I'm gripping Khun Choem's arm, leaning part of my leaden weight on her, slowing her down too. And every few seconds, there's a searing pain in my stomach; a sword stuck into me to slash me open. I have to stop. I need to breathe. As I muster the courage and step forward, another contraction gashes me from the front. I dig my nails into Khun Choem's arm. "Aaah!" she screams, "Aaah! Wanessa, *jep! Jep!*" (You're hurting me!)"

I don't mean to, but I've never been in such agony. Crippling, stabbing, burning pain that makes me want to collapse onto my hands and knees and crawl the rest of the way. Khun Choem is urging me on now. Saying it's not much further to the gates. But that distance stretches out before me like it's miles away. The heat stays close, breathing its vapour on me, making every step so much harder to take. And after what seems like hours of dragging and clawing and shuffling, I'm finally there.

A battered Toyota bakkie skids to a halt in front of me. Metal bars surround the back. A leather canvas is attached and several female prisoners called *kongkangs* for their masculine, sinewy build, jump out. They grasp my limbs like abattoir workers and load me into the back. I'm positioned between the steel thighs of a short, fat officer, propped up for my potholed journey to parenthood. The surface I sit on is bare and ridged. And when the gravel flies beneath the tyres, my body vibrates with every bump, crashes downwards into every hole in the surface, is thrust forward and back each time the brakes screech to a halt.

Lying there, latched between the officer's legs, the pain gets worse. I grab her hand and slap it to my stomach, moving it around in circles. Then I take her hand and clamp it to my back. She massages me this way for the rest of the journey. This trip is agonisingly long. "How long till we get there?" I keep asking. And she says "*Pepdio, pepdio!*" (Not far!) which means nothing to me.

But, finally, it looms before us. The massive white King's Hospital. I feel a rush of hope. One of the wardens brings me a wheelchair and wheels me into the building. This is the first time in months I've left the prison without going to court. I suddenly feel free. Like I've made it back to civilisation. This is a civilian hospital where ordinary people go. And after all this time, I'm among them again.

My brown prison uniform marks me as an offender, sets me apart from these good people who are suddenly afraid of me. And for just one second, I forget my pain, because it's overshadowed by shame. I'm put on a bench where I'll have to wait for a doctor.

A little Thai girl, about six years old, smiles at me, then laughs. It moves me. But her mother calls her back and holds her close.

Other people look at me like a criminal, start shifting away from me. I swallow hard. I want to tell them I'm actually innocent. But it's begun to sound so stupid these days. Today my body is sore, but my heart is aching. I sit here among strangers. No family. No friends who love me. And my child is about to enter the world, not knowing that literally all we have is each other. My mother and sisters would be frantic, fussing over me, encouraging me. But my mother doesn't have a clue that she's about to become a grandmother.

I'm taken to another room where I sit opposite a young Thai man. He's nervous and jittery. Behind him, a woman is giving birth. It must be his wife. He starts speaking to me in Thai, looking at me strangely, agitated. I shake my head to show him I don't understand. But he waves his hands in the air. He dashes down the corridor and runs back, pointing at his legs and then at mine. I look down and see a stream of blood flooding my legs.

A nurse bolts in, grabs me and pulls me into a ward where three Thai ladies are lying with their legs wide open, their feet strapped to the metal bars of the bed. "I clean you now," she says and gives me an enema. Then she shows me the ladies room and gives me a white hospital gown to change into. I can't wait to shed this filthy brown convict uniform and replace it with this starchy white gown that'll make me look like all the others.

In the bathroom, I lean over my massive belly and try to clean the blood off my legs. But it keeps coming. An unstoppable flow. I put the hospital gown on hastily, knotting it tightly at the back. And in the mirror, there's this face. Pale. Ashen and wide-eyed. I don't know this woman staring back at me. And suddenly I'm a little girl. I burst into tears. I cry for my mother, for my freedom, for the betrayal I've suffered. For all the harrowing things I've had to bear in prison. And through my tears I curse Felix. "Fuck you, Felix, I hate you! I hate you!" I yell, as though he's standing there. I slam myself against the wall behind me and slide down, spent. The blood streams. And I sob. I sob till I'm shaking so hard, I can't breathe.

I grab the showering hose, turn the cold water on full and douse myself. The gown is soaked. I stand under the falling water for a long time. I need it to chill me. To drain the last droplet of bitterness from me. But when I turn the water off and stand in front of the mirror again, I look maddened. I hate what I see. I bang my head against the mirror. "God help me, wherever you are," I whisper. "I'm scared. I'm so scared and I don't know what to do…"

I grab at the walls to steady myself. I look like I've escaped from a mental asylum, the wild look in my eyes, my hair scraggly. People in the corridors stare, then look away. And the nurse is so angry with me for soiling this gown she gave me. She makes me strip down and gives me another gown to wear. Then, she rushes me off to an empty delivery room. I'm followed into the room by a doctor and sixteen students, who've been brought there to watch me give birth. One student straps my legs to the metal bars of the bed. Another comes over to take my blood. But she can't find a vein. Eventually, I grab the needle and jab it in myself.

The pain has reached such a raging pitch now that I feel it could almost kill me. I shriek. I demand they give me something to curb it. I want to fight them. But I haven't eaten since early yesterday. I have no reserves left. And in this position, flat on my back with my legs strapped down, no pillow under my head, my lungs feel crushed. It's a struggle to get air in. And I can't waste these tiny, precious breaths on shouting anymore.

The nurse is standing over me. "You must push. Push now!" But I'm trying and it's as though she can't see that. "I can't breathe…" I tell her between short, shallow breaths. "It's difficult to lie… flat on my back… strapped in like this! Please… Please give me a pillow…" She shakes her head. I try to pull myself up by grabbing onto my legs. But she slaps my hands away and shouts, "Dirty – no touch!"

And then, this crowd surrounding me in a half-moon, suddenly begins humming in unison. It's an eerie sound, sinister and cultish. I feel like a human sacrifice spread out on their altar. It frightens me. I ask them, "Why are you singing?"

"We hum to make child go to toilet, for poo come out. Maybe if we hum, you want go toilet," one student explains. "Then you push baby out. If you feel you want go toilet, push. Push for baby come out."

But I can't anymore. I'm giving up. "Push!" the nurse says again. "It not good for the baby inside so long!" But when she sees I can't go on, she fixes one hand on either side of me and suddenly climbs on top of me, her face just centimetres from mine. "I help you push," she says, looking me directly in the eye. She positions her strong hands under my breasts, just where my stomach begins to rise. And she presses with such force that I feel something break. There's a warm gushing between my legs. It floods the sheets beneath me. My waters have broken.

"Okay, Wanessa, you push!" she says. "Push now!" She's suspended over me, her eyes full of hope. And somewhere in me, there is this anger, this aggression that I know I can channel to get my baby out. I grab hold of the girl standing on my right-hand side and ram my head into her stomach, screaming. She's shocked and a bit scared but she stands there, knowing it's what I have to do to get this baby out. The nurse continues pressing my stomach hard, forcing, crushing, squeezing. And then I feel it. A perfect sphere between my legs. My baby's head, waiting to emerge. I feel it trying to push forward to break through, but nothing happens beyond this. I'm beginning to panic, afraid that my baby is stuck there.

"You too small," the doctor cries out. "We cut." A second later, the coldness of the blade tears into my skin and I scream. "Okay, Wanessa, push!" the nurse says again. I close my eyes and clench every muscle in my body and bear down. But nothing happens. "We cut more – you too small," the doctor says again. And suddenly I don't care anymore how much he butchers me down there. I'm only afraid of what will happen to my precious child. The blade slices into me again. I give one final thrust. My last, my deepest push, just as she slams into me from above, and forces the mound of my stomach down. I feel my child slip through.

The nurse lifts her up and smiles. It's a girl. Born at 11:42am on

31 October 1994, weighing in at 3½ kilograms. She's silent until the doctor slaps her into life. But even then, she whimpers rather than cries. I hardly get to see her before they take her away, so I can deliver the afterbirth. The nurse reaches into me, wrenches it out. It's like liver, purple and jelly-like. She thumps it down so hard, it splatters blood on the wall.

They thread a needle and stitch me up – no anaesthetic, even though I beg for something to deaden the pain. Thirteen stitches should be child's play for a hardened criminal. I jerk, I wail, I grit my teeth as they thread the needle through my frayed flesh and yank the thread taut. Then it's over. The last stitch sewn in this tapestry of pain. But it's throbbing even harder on the inside. I've just given birth to a baby who, in my country, would be called a "born free" – a child stripped of the anguish, the indignity, the chains of apartheid. But my daughter is different. Her nursery will be a prison cell, her lullaby the King's Song, her cot a cold hard floor. This child that I have spent two days wrestling into the world – she has been born in shackles.

CHAPTER 14

Prison mom

Felicia is tiny and delicate. A powder-scented petal blown off the mother flower. She gives off a smell of such innocence, such helplessness when I hold her close. This is all I've been doing for hours since I've returned to Lard Yao – snuggling her in the crook of my arm, dusting her soft skin with feather kisses, drinking in every detail of her perfect face. She gazes at me with curiosity and affection through her liquid chocolate eyes, a pixie, cocooned in this pink blanket so tight it's almost a second skin. The doctors tell me she's healthy. But I still hand her to Elise nervously, asking her to count my baby's fingers and toes. Elise is delighted to report everything is as it should be.

A crowd of mothers and pregnant women swamp me in the hospital room. They're all dying to see this little bundle who kept me awake with her kicking at night. All these women who began as strangers are by my side, celebrating this milestone in my life. They ooh and aah over Felicia while she gurgles happily at all the attention. I revel in it too. I think of myself in the King's Hospital a few days ago, watching all the families of those new mothers stream in. Flowers and fruit baskets and cards and balloons and laughter echo through the ward while Felicia and I sit there alone, not one well-wisher, not one word of congratulations, as though every other baby born that day is a blessing, but mine.

Now I have one human being I can actually call family, and she's close by. At the hospital, they send a student to me to draw up a birth certificate. They ask me what I've named her. "Felicia," I say, "Felicia Goosen."

"Same surname?" she asks. "Yes," I say confidently. "Felicia Minah Goosen. Minah, after my mother."

The last few hours have left me feeling vulnerable. It's hard giving birth among strangers and having them nurse you in the absence of your flesh-and-blood loved ones. After I'm stitched and cleaned, I'm wheeled into a small room and put onto another bed. I'm so cold – it's freezing in here. I feel like I'm still in labour. And I'm trembling, drawing my limbs close to me to get warm. I ask the nurses for a blanket but they tell me, "This a low-class hospital", so there are none. "We put lights on you," they say. And they place two lights on either side of me that begin to cast a lukewarm glow. I don't want lights. But I surrender to them anyway. Let the warmth of them thaw me, penetrate me. And through my tears, I watch blurred reunions in the beds around me where new mothers are worshipped and their babies doted upon. It would be wonderful to have my mother here, but Jacky will have given birth by now and I'm sure she needs my mother more.

An hour passes. I'm moved to a general ward. It's been about a day since I've eaten and I'm starving. The nurse brings me a steaming cup of Ovaltine that flows past my cracked lips and floods my mouth, my throat, my stomach, a river of warm, malty, sweet, sticky deliciousness. I beg for three more cups and lick them down to the last drop. But by lunch, I can't stomach the fried eggs and rice I'm given. I fall asleep.

At 4pm, I'm shaken awake. It's time to go back to Lard Yao. They bring Felicia to me, all wrapped in her candy-pink towel. She's fast asleep. I cuddle her for just a few moments before the prison guards arrive. The old Toyota van pulls up again. Everything will play out in reverse. An officer takes Felicia so she can sit in front and hold my baby, while I travel in the back again.

The stitches between my legs are tender. This time, I sit on my own, supporting myself, trying to lessen the impact of the bumps, the potholes and the jaggedness of the road surface like a grater beneath me. I feel a jabbing pain between my legs, needles in my skin, the slow unpicking, tearing, loosening of these stitches, the tugging of my flesh as they jerk apart, the slow-forming scabs beginning to flake off. I jam my legs together. Clench my bum, my thighs, my knees. "Oh God please help me survive this," I pray. But the bottom of the van slams against me, hammers my pelvis from below with such force that I'm convinced I'm bleeding again.

By the time we reach Lard Yao, I'm in such agony I can't get out of the van. The *kongkangs* spring into action, trying to help me clamber to my feet. But I can't stand. My stitches are stretching taut. I take slower steps. I lean on these muscular women and try to steady myself. But a weakness grips me. My legs buckle and a dark blanket is thrown over me.

I wake up on a hospital bed in Lard Yao after fainting outside. And here's Felicia, lying stiffly rolled in the pink blanket, at the foot of my bed. She starts to cry and it's suddenly too much for me. I don't know that I can look after her. So instead of comforting her, I cry too. I sob aloud, "I can't handle this! I don't know how to raise a child…" My crying drowns out Felicia's. I grab a towel and I scream into it. I hide my face from her, so Felicia doesn't see my madness. Another prisoner I don't know comes rushing in and begs me to calm down for the baby's sake. "What you feel she feel too," she tells me. And at that moment, Elise comes in to check on us both to see if we're settling in. She talks to me, reasons with me and reminds me that I have to be strong for this little girl. When I look at Felicia again, she's fast asleep.

I have very little maternal instinct and the slightest thing that goes wrong throws me into a panic. When Felicia starts to make a strange grunting sound, I realise she may be struggling to breathe. But I have no one to ask for help. The nurses tell me Felicia must've swallowed some amniotic fluid because she was in the birth canal for too long. As they're explaining this to me, my prisoner nurse, Dowa Chat, walks in. She heads straight for Felicia and listens to this strange sound she's making. Dowa Chat bends down, clamps her mouth over Felicia's tiny nose and sucks hard. Then she turns her head away and spits a ball of phlegm onto the floor. I'm both grateful and sickened by it, mostly because I know I couldn't have done it myself. After that, they drain her lungs often.

Felicia also suffers from colic, scrunching her little face in pain and pulling her legs up to her tummy. She cries for hours and hours and hours, mostly overnight. I somehow manage to pacify her during the daylight hours. But at night I'm ratty and impatient. "I'm tired, can't you be quiet, just for one moment? I need to sleep!" I shout at her. Later, the guilt sets in. When she quietens down, I say sorry to her and ask her to forgive me.

For the first few days, I have no milk and Elise breastfeeds Felicia until I start producing my own milk. When I offer her my breast, she explores my nipple, latches and drinks thirstily. But after three months pass, she no longer wants my milk. She spits it out and cries. It's probably because of my poor nutrition. The mothers of infants at Lard Yao mostly eat a duck egg and water-logged rice. Occasionally, I get some cucumber and tomato soup or a marrow-like vegetable they call *fak* cooked with a small fish, head and tail still attached.

After Felicia's birth, the cold creeps into my body and stays there. October in Thailand is cooler because of the monsoon rains, but it never really gets cold because the country is so close to the equator. Despite that, nothing I drink or eat warms me. The water in the bath trough feels icy. I have to clean my stitches in this dirty water and I pray I won't end up with an infection, especially because it throbs so hard between my legs after I bath each day. I don't get an infection but it takes a long time before my wounds heal. I do my best never to bath Felicia with the chilly trough water. When I'm forced to, she cries uncontrollably. So whenever I can, I steal hot water from the flasks the nurses give us to make the baby's bottles with and I bath her with this.

I'm still worried about how I will clothe her and be able to afford the most basic toiletries she needs. Soon after Felicia's birth, I write to Aunty Rushda to tell her all about the newest little member of our family. She writes back to say she's relieved and delighted and she's sent a baby hamper full of clothes, blankets, nappies, Vaseline, formula and baby powder. These are all the necessities I haven't been able to afford. I'm so impatient for the parcel to arrive. But when it does, it lands in the hands of some embassy officials who don't bring it to me. First they say the rats have chewed the contents. Then they say they're washing some of the baby clothes that were soiled. Eventually, all I end up with are a small pink baby brush and twelve disposable nappies.

The rest of Felicia's clothes come from missionaries who visit the prison. Rachel and Michael of the Nazarene Church have been supporting me for many months now. They bring lots of clothes and large quantities of formula to the prison for Felicia. And two generous South African Airways hostesses who've read about me in the newspapers bring something special for both of us each time they stop over in Bangkok.

I feel it's important for me to have Felicia baptised, especially because of the surroundings I'm raising her in. So one morning, outside the library, a small table with a pink cloth and a jug of water is set up. Rachel and Michael are allowed to enter the prison and conduct this small service where we ask for Felicia's protection. The guards give Michael some iced water to bless and when he sprinkles it on Felicia's forehead to make the sign of the cross there, my child starts bawling and doesn't stop! It's obvious that I'm a lot happier about Felicia's baptism than she is!

A Nigerian inmate, Mariam, gets her friend on the outside to buy me some baby clothes. They're put in my name when they're brought into the prison and I'm so grateful to her for the package. But soon after it arrives, Mariam demands the strappy pair of black and blue rubber-soled shoes back. I can't understand why. She has no children here. Then I realise there must've been something illegal hidden in those shoes. And if the officers had found drugs in them, I'd be facing even more drug charges and a heftier sentence.

But despite the many ups and downs, I see Felicia's birth as a miracle. How is it that a little person, so beautifully formed, so perfectly built, could emerge out of my body? Despite all I went without during my pregnancy, Felicia is thriving. She's a magnet who attracts all kinds of attention, and Lisa Goslin is one of those drawn to her.

She's an American with a life sentence, who'll probably only serve about eight years at Lard Yao because her government will soon ask for her to be sent home. We strike up a friendship that grows into a deep bond. Lisa is very well educated and worked as a broker before she was arrested.

But she's also a strange contradiction. On the one hand, she loves to stare in the mirror and often draws on a bright pair of red lips. On the other hand, she's battling a weight problem and low self-esteem. She's a caring, patient human being who loves the innocence of children and relates to them in such an open way.

Lisa often helps me to take care of Fifi, arriving early in the morning to babysit. She and Felicia have entire conversations that no one else understands. Lisa's and my friendship matures like slow-brewed tea. We almost share Felicia because Lisa comes to feel such a personal responsibility for her. She becomes my little girl's second mother. We share our lives, our pain, our brief moments of happiness – as much as Lard Yao will afford us.

My Rasta friend, Olivia, is also close to me. And when she sees me struggling with the basics of motherhood, she gives me a book to help me along. It's old-fashioned and outdated. But when you know nothing, Dr Spock will do. My mind often flits back to Jacky. In her letter, Aunty Rushda tells me about my beautiful niece, baby Jocelyn, born at the end of September. She and Felicia are almost exactly a month apart. What joy my sister and I would've had in raising our girls together. I wonder how Jacky is managing with the demands of a newborn.

I've managed to put this off for months now. But the day soon comes when the Thai courts can wait no longer. So on 1 December 1994, I'm among the group of prisoners loaded into the back of the van and taken back to the magistrate's court. This is my ninth appearance before this court and still I understand no more than I did the first time. I leave without being told the outcome.

But when I return to Lard Yao, Nola is waiting for me. She's an Australian prisoner in her late forties who now works as a prison translator. I find her in the open-plan office, furnished with four desks, two of them in the middle of the room. I sit on a chair while she prefers to sit on the floor. While I wait, I picture the officer at the airport, pointing to his poster, telling me "heroin is death sentence". I imagine what it would be like to stand before a firing squad with their guns cocked. I wonder what it would be like for Felicia to grow up without a mother. But I'm astonishingly calm.

Nola is sympathetic when she fixes her big green eyes on me. "Vanessa, you were given a death sentence, but because you're a first-time offender and a young mother, they commuted your sentence to life." At first, I sit there, shocked. Then I walk away, my eyes falling on every detail of Lard Yao. The compound's high walls, the factories, the dining hall, the water trough, the prison cells. This is my home for a hundred years. I will live out the rest of my days here. And I will eventually die here.

There's a woman in her eighties jailed here, shrivelled and bent over, a wrinkled question mark with a watery film over her eyes. And I picture myself in sixty years, just like her. My leathery form sardined among all the young flesh on the cell floor. I don't want to be her. But a hundred years is a long time. Seventeen days later, on 18 December, it's my birthday. And on this day I turn twenty-two years old, all I can think is: *Vanessa, from today onwards, you only have seventy-eight years left in Lard Yao.* And that thought leaves me so shocked and devastated, that I sit in the nursery the whole day, alone with Felicia, sobbing.

Six months later, I appeal my sentence, but I'm given life in prison yet again. My friends tell me it could've been so much worse – I could've got the death sentence. But I know death would be the easy way out of this. The pain only lasting a few short minutes compared to an entire lifetime. Right now, Felicia is the only reason to go on living. And I suppose as I gave her life, she has given me life too, sparing me from the firing squad.

I receive my prisoner ID card. It lists all my details – my name, surname, age, date of arrest, release date and case information. The card is colour-coded depending on the length of your sentence. My card is yellow. We wear our ID cards at all times. And each morning, as I pin it to my chest, I look hard at this badge of dishonour. The shame shadows me. I can taste the bitterness at the back of my tongue. I'm Vanessa Goosen. Just another lifer at Lard Yao.

CHAPTER 15

Ticking clock

A few months after Felicia's birth, I'm told there's a visitor waiting to see me. At first, I don't recognise him. But then I look closer and I see his pockmarked face and I can't believe that my Angel Officer has come to see me. I'm thrown back to my arrest at the airport, those chaotic hours in the interrogation room when I screamed and screamed and he was the only one who came. He touched my shoulder and took my statement and wrapped his jersey round my wrists to hide my disgrace. He showed me such humanity that day and I'm happy to see him again.

"Why have you come here?" I ask him. And all he says is, "Wanessa, I'm sorry. I'm sorry I couldn't do more. If it was in my hands, I would've let you go. I knew you were innocent."

I'm shocked. His words move me, bring tears to my eyes. Someone in the system believes me, although we both know he can't do anything about it.

"Can I please see your child?" he asks. He's brought her a gift of toiletries. I bring Felicia in and he looks at her with such admiration. Maybe he's thinking that she doesn't belong here. And neither do I. My Angel Officer wishes us the best, says he's sorry again and leaves knowing he can still do nothing to save us.

We go back to mark the passing of time in prison. Many inmates don't. Why bother, when you have to live out the rest of your days here anyway? The clocks move sluggishly. Time stretches out before you, a ball of raw dough under a rolling pin, expanding flat and vast, so much bigger than when you started out. One day blurs restlessly into the next, passing with such monotony – the death of a handful of sunsets; the birth of an armful of new days holding only the promise of staleness. Each day smells, tastes, of the previous day's sourness. And when you're a mother in a Thai prison, there's only one thing that wakes you up to time's brisk march: having a child living with you behind bars.

Felicia begins as a newborn who drinks from me and screams from colic and flies through the thin Thai diapers like she's paging through a book. Weeks pass and she learns to smile and respond to me and from then on, time breaks into a slow run, gaining speed as it passes. My life takes on a new pace because there's so much to do for Felicia. In the morning, if she's awake at 5am, I stretch my legs out, place her on them and clean her with what little running water is available from a tap in our cell.

Once the cell door flings opens at 6am, a relay race begins. I hand her over to Mariam, who's able to care for her while I rush out to shower and wash Felicia's clothes at the same time. Mariam is the tall, loud Nigerian woman, who slowly begins to step into the role of Felicia's nanny while I'm away. After I've showered, Mariam passes Fifi back to me while she goes to shower. I hand her back to Mariam to fetch breakfast, and after Felicia's drunk her milk from me and we've eaten, I rush out to work at the factory. Felicia spends much of her time in-between at the baby's nursery – a small blue-and-white room where all the newborns are cared for while their mothers are at work.

Mariam is from the Hosea tribe of Nigeria. It breaks her heart that Felicia and I have so little. She begins visiting us and, in time, develops a real bond with Fifi. Mariam's on hand every morning, lunch time and evening to help with Fifi. This is really a godsend because in prison, a mother can't possibly manage without the help of others and there's little time to rest. Our babies need cleaning and care. There are bottles to sterilise and clothes to wash. Their clothes are hung up to dry in a shared hanging space and if we don't stay there and watch them, they get stolen.

My working day at the factory begins at 8am and I dash out at roughly eleven, to breastfeed my baby. I return to work until lunchtime when Felicia's due for another feed. At tea-time, round about 3pm, I breastfeed Felicia again and return to the factory until it shuts down. There are just over two hours left before the day wraps up, during which we must pack our bags that we're taking into the cells overnight, leave them there to be inspected, eat and clean ourselves and our babies. At 5:30pm, it's lockdown. We're patted down as we re-enter our hovels. The TV's on from seven to ten in the evening. And that marks the end of another day at Lard Yao.

This frenzied routine slowly causes me to unravel. There are days when I struggle to meet all the demands of a prison mom. Days when I feel my head is bursting from all the things I have to remember. If I forget just one task, Felicia suffers as a result and the pressure on me to never forget a single thing is too much. I cry, I curse, become moody and irritable. I lose my appetite. A nurse tells me that I'm suffering from postnatal depression. I don't know what this means but when she asks me, "You want sleep in hospital?" I say no, because I know I have to take care of my daughter.

The days lie piled up in a heap that decays into months. And Felicia is no longer the infant who slept for hours and was happy to be rocked asleep in my arms. After a violent fever, her first teeth have already come shooting out of her gums. She's crawling away from babyhood with speed to become a toddler and she's spitting out all her first words in Thai. I blink for a moment and she's suddenly a year old – one whole year! We celebrate her first birthday with a big group of prisoners and wardens alike. Officers who shed their severe looks to sing her happy birthday. Inmates who've forgotten their own pain for a moment so they can bless my child with their good wishes. Felicia loves her cake, drinks up all the attention, fawns over everyone who's brought her a present.

I'm so grateful that she's made it this far. There's so much that can go wrong with a child in a prison – especially in that first year. For a start, these structures are built for adults only. There's nothing child-friendly about them, so prison babies must adapt as they grow and explore. There are no doctors here either and disease is rife even among the other children, so I end up going to extremes to keep Felicia healthy. There are also women in this prison serving sentences for sexual crimes against children and this makes me vigilant, paranoid even, about Felicia's safety as she comes into contact with more of the inmates.

Life in here will never be like life on the outside, but I try to make it as "normal" for Felicia as possible. I take her to the single swing and slide outside the nursery and pretend we're in a park. I play games with her. We talk and sing songs. I let her enjoy the few shared toys available to kids in prison because the officers mostly keep them on display instead of allowing the children to play with them. And as her level of understanding increases, I begin to teach her letters of the alphabet and colours. Sometimes we page through magazines together and I use these as a tool to try and drive home the concepts of letters and colours. Felicia is bright and sucks up everything she's taught. She begins to show a real maturity, not least because she spends all her time with adults these days.

What I don't realise is that the days of Mariam's help will soon be over. When Felicia is a-year-and-a-half old, Mariam sits me down and tells me she's fallen in love with me. I'm shocked, because I had no idea she felt this way. Mariam and I have a fight in which terrible things are said. And I take Felicia out of her care. I leave my job to take care of Felicia myself.

But being out of work makes me feel unproductive. So besides looking after Felicia, I volunteer to teach aerobics classes. This could be a way of restoring my own health and teaching other women that we need not give up on our bodies, even in a place like this. At that time, all the mothers are moved from our building, Poisy, to another one called Pathai. And the woman in charge of our building, Me Wee asks me if she can look after Felicia.

She's a former officer arrested for fraud, but she's respected and feared. We're all terrified by her stern looks. She doesn't hesitate to hit and punish those she feels are out of line. I'm not sure I can trust this woman with my child. But I discover that she really is very fond of children. She babysits Felicia during the aerobics classes, so I can watch them both. And she shows my daughter real love. I begin to trust her and she takes care of Felicia in the morning, lunch time and evening.

The other officer who grows to adore Felicia is Khun Su. She's in charge of the area between Factory 3 and Factory 4. Khun Su spoils Felicia with new clothes and all sorts of luxuries from outside that the *lanka* doesn't stock. Felicia always brings her treats to me first because she understands that I don't want her to eat anything without being sure of what's in it first. I teach her that not just anyone is allowed to touch her, especially because the Thais in prison seem to think nothing of touching a child's private parts.

The Thai language rolls off Felicia's tiny tongue. The officers love it and bend the rules for her all the time. They offer Felicia food after lockdown at 5:30pm, pushing it through the bars. We share it although the adults aren't allowed to eat in the cells at all. And when the TV goes off at 10 o'clock at night, Felicia screams *"Khun ka purt tv n aka!"* (Officer please put the TV on!) And much to the delight of the other mothers, it's switched on again. Felicia also warns us when there's going to be a raid on our cells. This gives me time to hide all the illegal objects I've managed to sneak in – a knife made out of a sharpened metal spoon to slice my vegetables with, a bag, pyjamas and a bible cover that an inmate in the factory made especially for me.

The children are allowed a small snack that can be taken into the cells in their bags overnight. One evening, an American friend of mine, Touche, smuggles in a snack between her legs. When Touche is searched, the officer finds nothing. A few days later, Felicia tucks a bag of Mamma noodles between her legs but doesn't say a word about it to me. We line up to be patted down and Felicia waltzes in without being found out. Once she's in the cell, she pulls out the noodles and shouts to the officer, "Look, you didn't see I had these noodles in my panty!"

The officer tells her to hand them over, but she refuses. "No I will not! You didn't find it so now I'm going to eat it!" I laugh out loud and tell Touche she's setting a bad example for my daughter!

This is what Felicia brings to my life and the bland lives of others around me. Rare moments of happiness in which we forget where we are and how we got here. My child is a gash of light that breaks through the roof of this dingy prison and floods it with her innocence. Laughter and kindness seem to follow her everywhere. Prisoner and guard love her the same. She makes us all believe there's something human about one another.

It warms my heart to watch Felicia grow. Each little milestone floods me with pride. But I also know what it means and that's why every move towards her newfound independence scares me. Every day she is older, she takes one step closer to that prison door. To a world outside that she doesn't know and that doesn't know her and won't take kindly to the child of a convict. I shove it out of my mind. I tell myself that day is still months away and I won't let myself think about it until it's almost upon me. Upon us.

There's nothing I can do to stop this whirlpool of time that's sucked her in, spinning faster all the time. I must just love her as much as I can, love her enough for the years ahead, while we're still together.

Her second birthday crash-lands on top of us. And we gather again for this all-adult kiddies' party because there are no other children Felicia's age left at Lard Yao. Officers and inmates, we all cluster round and sing, each one drawn by the magnetism of this child. Felicia doesn't understand this birthday-party-turned-on-its-head without a specially iced cake or a jumping castle or brand-new presents from shops. Her gifts bear the mark of handmade things: hanging threads, off-cuts and mismatched colours. But all she knows is she's loved. She counts her gifts and squeals with excitement and flings herself forward to hug the givers. And while I'm happy that I have a child who can make so many hearts glad, mine is breaking. My days with her are numbered. They'll flee just as every day of the last two years has. And the morning will come when she will take her light, her love for me, away from this prison. And I know, those dark days before her birth, they will come back to haunt me again.

CHAPTER 16

Ten kisses

About six months before Felicia's third birthday, Lard Yao's officials suddenly change their policy regarding children. Mothers locked up in Thai jails who've previously been allowed to keep their children with them until the age of three, may now only keep them there up to the age of one. A suitable guardian must be found so the child can be sent to that person at the age of one. If a caregiver can't be found, the child will be thrust into an orphanage. I'm terrified by what this means for Felicia. And as I predict, just days later, I'm called into one of the administration offices where they're waiting to tell me what I already know. Felicia must go. I've been expecting it, but their words still slam into me like a bus. But I stand there, angry and defiant. "No," I spit back. "You won't take her away from me until she turns three." And I storm out.

I need to delay Felicia's departure for as long as possible because I'm still full of hope that if I'm granted a pardon by the King of Thailand, my child and I will leave this place together. These officials will never understand what it means to raise a child in prison. Every moment of every day is spent doing something for that little person's benefit. Even when I'm working in the factory away from Felicia, I'm trying to scrape together the equivalent of R100 for three months' work just to support her.

I give her everything I can in this place of scarcity. And for the time that Felicia's been with me, I've loved her enough to make up for the absence of a father and a family. I've kept her in the best health possible. I've taught her as much as her young mind will absorb for now. I've protected her fiercely, so she's come to no harm. That is the irony of raising her here. Part of me now feels like prison is somehow slightly less dangerous than the world outside these walls. Of course I want Felicia to know freedom. But outside of here, I won't be there to protect her. And despite what Lard Yao is doing to me, Felicia's experience has been so different. She's drawn love from the hearts of strangers. Smiles from the cement-faced. She's a secure, happy child despite her circumstances, because she knows nothing else. And – she's saved me. Stopped me from splintering into pieces. Helped to keep me strong and alert and alive. I can't imagine living without her.

The officers tolerate my stubbornness for about two more months after that first meeting. But by the end of those eight weeks, they feel they've given me enough grace. The next time I'm called in, they seem so much more determined. They want me to get Felicia out of here immediately. I know I can't hold them off for much longer. So I plead with them to give me more time. "You know I'm a foreigner," I say. "It'll be impossible for me to find someone to foster my child and expect that person to fly to Thailand and take her home straight away…" They sigh as though they've already bent the rules so far back, they could snap. "Take little more time. But organise…" they say. And I run out of there, flushed with relief that I've managed to delay this one more time, although I don't know for how long.

That feeling only lasts two months, because on 31 August, exactly two months before Felicia's third birthday, they call me in for the third time. I stand there trembling. I have nothing to report on my progress with finding a family for her. I haven't done a thing, in the hope that somehow God will answer my prayers and melt these people's hearts so that they will let me keep my child here just a few months longer. But what they've called me for is to tell me Felicia must leave the prison on the morning of her third birthday.

I'm devastated. I burst out of that office without saying a word because I have nothing more to say to them. I've run out of excuses. I'm so angry with myself! How could I have allowed myself to believe that this could be put off forever? I've known for years now that Felicia would have to leave at some point but I've never prepared myself for it. Never once thought to myself, today's the day you'll start putting on some kind of emotional armour that'll stop you from falling to pieces the day she goes. Yes, I've feared it. Yes, I've got on my knees and prayed it would never happen. But prepare myself for it? Never. Worse than that, I haven't prepared my child for this. In her mind, this is the way it'll always be. Felicia and Mummy against the world. Now everything my daughter knows is about to start disintegrating around her.

If I'm angry with myself, then I'm enraged with God! "I prayed to you!" I cry out. "I asked you to please let me go home with my daughter. And whatever it is you want me to do in this prison, I'll do it for you. But I want to go home with my daughter!" I cry some more. I beg. But nothing changes. There's no burning bush or angel voices. Lard Yao gives and Lard Yao takes away. There'll be no exception with Felicia.

For the next month, I can't bring myself to tell anyone Felicia is leaving – not the officers taking care of her, not my friends, not Felicia herself. I need this time to absorb what's about to happen. To picture all of these surroundings, these people, my entire life in this prison without my child. Some nights, I drown myself to sleep in my own tears. Otherwise, I lie awake watching Felicia, savouring every last moment with her. I put my arms around her, even though I know she's not a child who's fond of being smothered in the heat of this jail cell. I need to do this. Wrap her in my arms, so I can remember one day what she felt like just before she was taken from me. But she gently nudges me away. "Mummy, move back onto your mat," she says in Thai. I used to find this irritation of hers so cute, so funny. Now it tears into me because I can feel the melting, the dripping away of these last days, like a candle I know will soon burn out, leaving just a short stub of cold memory behind.

Each day, I watch her, my little Thai-South African, speeding towards her third year of life. She speaks fluent Thai, she's so familiar with Thai culture. She knows nothing about South Africa, except what I've told her. She doesn't know its food or its people or any of its languages properly. How do I prepare her for this massive change? I can only sit with her and build up an image in her mind of what this new world called South Africa will look and smell and sound like. That's what I'll do. Make it sound like heaven outside of here, so she'll eventually be desperate to go. "There's hot water in South Africa," I tell her. "You know how we always shower out in the open with cold water?" And she nods, her big, brown eyes locked onto me. "Well, in South Africa, there's plenty of hot water and the shower's inside a house, and when you're finished having a shower there's a fluffy towel to put around you to make you feel nice and warm... And there's nice food. There are parks, wide open spaces, and lovely toys and lots of other children to play with." I haul out some magazines I've kept for exactly this moment and I show her the pictures. They're bright and colourful and brimming with smiling people. That's what South Africa looks like, Fifi," I say. And she believes me. I'm so relieved that she believes me. After I tell her this, the secret's out. She runs about telling everyone, "I'm going to South Africa! I'm going to South Africa!" And each time I hear it, there's just a small stab of pain, overshadowed by my child's joy at going to this wonderful place she deserves to call home.

My main worry is who exactly I will send her to. Aunty Rushda is divorced. My mother is sickly and in and out of hospital these days. Johnny, my friend from the police cells who took care of me and clothed and fed me before I went to Lard Yao, writes to me from Klong Prem next door. He says his mom is visiting him and she's happy to take Felicia to the United States with her. I'm grateful but I can't give her up to a complete stranger.

The only people who will qualify as foster parents in South Africa are a married couple. And when they hear that, Melanie, my childhood friend, and her husband, Hilton, come forward. I think of Melanie as a young girl growing up in Eldorado Park with me. She's loud and full of fun and once told me when we were just teenagers that she'd never let me down. Now I'm about to hold her to a promise we made when we were just girls. A promise that will make her my child's mother.

Part of me feels it's too much to ask of her. She and Hilton have their own lives now. They're a happily married couple living in the suburbs, in the south of Johannesburg, with their own little girl. Now, I'm asking them to derail their lives for me. To take in this little stranger I love, who doesn't know anything but prison life. But Melanie never breaks a promise. And Hilton, I've known him for years too. He's our close friend, Collette's cousin, and the boy I called an older brother on the streets of Eldorado Park for years. Melanie and Hilton have both known my mother since they were children. So they go to her and ask her if she would mind at all if they took Felicia in. My mother gives them her blessing. And that's what brings them to Thailand when I need them most.

In the last week of October, Melanie and Hilton visit us at Lard Yao every day. They try to get to know Felicia in the limited time we're all given together. They try to win Felicia over, make her laugh, make her feel that their own daughter, Lerell, will be a sister to her in the years to come. The guards open the door between us and Felicia rushes out to meet them while I sit behind the wire mesh watching her slowly slip out of my grasp. But I have complete trust in my friends and know she'll have a balanced life with them. They play with her, they try to talk to her but although she understands English, she only responds in Thai.

This makes me slightly anxious. How will she tell Melanie and Hilton what she needs? How will she relate to Melanie's daughter after hardly spending any time with other children? I have no answers. I only have seven short days to make my friends and my daughter a family and hope they stay that way for as long as I'm in prison.

The day of their last visit is 31 October 1997. It's Felicia's birthday. At 6am sharp, I'm summoned to the office to be reminded, as though it might've somehow slipped my mind, that my daughter must leave today. I still can't really believe it, because no matter how I've tried to prepare us all for this day, I still hold out some impossible hope that something will happen to make Felicia stay. But there'll be no miracles today.

Felicia's excited from the moment she opens her eyes. It's her birthday and in just a few hours she'll be heading for South Africa. My prison friends throw a small party for her and give her their handmade gifts as they've done each year before. I see how delighted she is with them. This is the moment I want to burn into my mind. Her round, happy face. Her joy at being spoilt with so many gifts even if they are the most basic toys a child could receive. But I can't watch for much longer. I leave her there to enjoy that moment without my sadness staining it. I go back to my cell with her gifts and I pack them along with all of Felicia's other belongings into a small bag.

It's time for Melanie and Hilton's last visit this week. I'm dreading it, willing the clocks to slow down because I know how this visit will end. They come in and we sit in the embassy room and I chat to them across the mesh. But in my mind there are only two people in the room. Felicia and me. The only focus of my attention is my baby, who's chatting away excitedly, playing with me as though this is just another ordinary day. And even though I try to fill each second to bursting with my happy words and silly jokes that make her laugh, the moment comes when I have to remind her that it's almost time to go. And it suddenly hits her. It hits her for what seems to be the first time, that yes, it is her birthday and she is going to this amazing place called South Africa. But she has to do it without me. And Felicia seems stung by this fact as though I've never mentioned it before. Now she shakes her head, says to me, "I'm not going to South Africa anymore."

"What?"

"I'm not going to South Africa anymore, Mummy."

Her words fall with a clatter between us. Melanie and Hilton walk away. Melanie's crying softly on the other side of the bars.

I don't know what to say. I try to talk Felicia into going. Remind her of all the pictures in the magazine. Remember, baby? Hot water. A bed. Warm bedsheets. Lots of toys. I'm rattling this off like a shopping list. Hoping just one image will hook her. And she'll go. But she looks so uninterested. So distracted and confused. "Felicia!" I want to shake her! I'm beginning to sound desperate and anxious. This visit ends in fifteen minutes. Just fifteen minutes! And the clock is ticking loudly. And the officers are looking at me. Eyeing me to see if I can pull this off. Because they've warned me that if my child doesn't walk out of this prison of her own free will at exactly 3pm, they will take her by force and they will dump her in a Thai orphanage.

I'm terrified! I beg her now. "Please! Please, Fifi! You have to go with Melanie and Hilton! Remember what we spoke about? Remember Fifi?" I remind her again. But she doesn't say a word. I'm choking up. I'm trying not to cry. I'm almost on the verge of breaking this ugly truth to her if it's the only thing that'll make her go. Of shattering her three-year-old innocence by shouting, don't you understand? You'll end up, just another lost child without *any* parents if you don't go right now?

But I can't.

I can't bring myself to say this to my little girl whose mind is so clouded over by the thought that she's leaving behind the only person who's never left her side.

I start praying silently, whispering under my breath. "Please God. Please! Make her say yes. Please make her agree to go with them! Please God. Help me to change her mind, please!"

I look at the clock and it's almost 3pm. The hand is marching with such finality. And it suddenly feels like I have the death sentence again and I'm standing in front of the firing squad with their rifles aimed at me and in half a minute I will be dead. But Felicia touches me. She looks at me and says, "Okay, I will go to South Africa. But you have to come too."

"I *will* come... soon," I say to her.

Felicia calls out to the officer. "Open the gate." And as it swings open, she walks out calmly. She calls all the officers round and says goodbye to them in turn. This prison has truly matured Felicia beyond her years.

On the other side, the officers shower her with gifts of teddy bears and all kinds of other toys – her birthday / going away presents. I can't deny that these women, for all the cruelty they're capable of, seem to possess a love for my child just as deep. The door shuts. And Felicia runs back to me again and again and again to kiss me goodbye through the wire mesh that separates us. I count ten kisses in all.

I can't hold back my tears any longer although one officer stands next to me, whispering to me not to cry. But it's Felicia who comes back one last time to dry my tears through the grille. "Don't cry, Mummy," she says. "You coming soon, Mummy, you promise?"

I see the expectation in her eyes. "I'm coming soon, baby," I say.

She turns and walks towards the main gate. And as it creaks open, the world suddenly floods in. This world of things she knows nothing about. It rushes at her so fiercely, doesn't give her one moment to steady herself. A car. A man. A busy street. She doesn't understand any of it. She begins to scream and scream from the depths of her soul. It's a sound I don't know. Have never heard pouring from my child's mouth ever before. But I know it's the sound of raw, jagged fear unleashed by my little girl on this huge world that must seem so much bigger without her mother standing beside her. I fall to my knees. I sob so hard, so violently, that the officer stands over me to shield Felicia from this last picture of her mother, a tear-stained heap on the prison floor. But Felicia never looks back. Her screaming becomes softer and dies away. There's the slamming of a car door. An engine snarls. And the one source of my life, my breath, my entire reason to live, is gone.

CHAPTER 17

Pardon

There's a violent fluttering in my eyelids as I try to prise them open. They're made of lead. Welded together by exhaustion. Drowsiness. A kind of paralysis that's taken me prisoner. I can feel she's there – this foreigner. And I want to open my eyes to look at her. But the urge to do anything, the strength to do it, has drained out of me. I must rally every cell in my body, use every last pocket of air in my flattened lungs to break through this glue that keeps my eyelids sealed.

I breathe in slowly, my lungs like two punctured balloons, letting in a wheezy breath. Then I push, I force, I punch, I bang on these eyelids like two prison doors, to break the seals, even if only for one moment. The afternoon sun surges in, a blaring floodlight in the soft jelly of my eyes. And I have to let them fall shut again. But in the split second I've wrenched them open, I've caught sight of her. This foreigner standing over me. Over what's left of me. This shell of a body that's leaked all its contents. That lies in this hospital bed limp, hollow, echoey, sucked down to the bone.

"You can't do this, Vanessa…" she says. "You're a very selfish person."

I would laugh if I could. If I could just get these tired muscles around my mouth to turn upwards. What does she know about me? About how I came to be this way? What gives her the right to call me selfish? After eight years, eight elastic years stretching taut like the belly of a pregnant woman, haven't I earned the right to be a bit selfish?

It's been 2 920 days since I walked into Lard Yao, screaming my innocence in the face of anyone who would listen. But no one has. There's this massive crater of land that should be a vast lake. But it's empty down to the last drop, so its rocky, sandy surface is naked. And strangely, a hosepipe lies at the very edge like a snake, turned off, except for the rhythmic falling every few seconds of just one drop over the side. One drop swallowed so fast by the thirsty sand, it's too small, too unimportant to make any difference. And I have to live with the knowledge that only when this lake is full one day, I'll go home.

It's been two months now, since I caved in and came to lie in this bed. Two months since I let the last eight horrible years crush me like a cockroach under a shoe after I'd spent so many years scurrying away from reality. Fighting. Believing there's always some hope I'll get out of here and go home to Felicia. On the day she leaves Lard Yao five years earlier a chunk of me is gouged out and sent with her. But even though I collapse and cry and I'm broken to pieces and her leaving fills me with hate for this system, I still have to believe there's a way out of this and no test of faith can last forever.

In the meantime, I send cards and letters. Three a week. I draw childish pictures with bright-coloured pens. My hand on the left side of the page labelled "Mommy's hand". Hers on the right labelled "Fifi's hand". And that's how I touch her across the distance. "Don't forget I love you" or "Mommy is coming home soon!" I pencil into the margins. And at some point I realise it's time I stopped sending these "baby" letters home now because she's no longer the three-year-old who walked out of here. I miss all her milestones – every birthday, her first day at school, her first race on Sports Day, her school concerts.

Melanie helps me to stay in touch with Felicia's life. She documents everything for me, including what happens right after Felicia leaves the prison. Mrs Holmes, the Filipino missionary, and her American husband throw a party for Felicia at their home in Bangkok. They raise a big banner saying "Happy birthday!" Felicia runs around there and tastes real freedom for the first time. She has a real birthday cake with three candles and she and Lerell climb up onto the table to blow them out together.

But Melanie tells me other things that disturb me. Like how, when they pull away from Lard Yao with Felicia, they have to constantly stop the car for her to vomit at the side of the road – she's never been in a car before. Melanie writes about the journey home too. And I see Felicia crying throughout the flight, begging them to stop the plane, while the other passengers stare, annoyed at this little girl who won't shut up about this scary flying machine. Melanie sends me a picture of the party she throws for Felicia at home, where my daughter sits completely alone, quietly paging through a magazine while everyone else chats happily around her. I just have to trust that Felicia will get over her fear of the telephone, the swimming pool and all men except Hilton.

Melanie is fighting battles of her own. Hilton has to wash Felicia, clean and dress her all the time because she will hardly let Melanie touch her. In Felicia's mind, Melanie is the monster who's taken her away from me. Who's trying to take my place. I know Felicia's afraid she'll never see me again. That these three years we shared at Lard Yao will blur and run, like love letters in the rain. Melanie cries so hard at Felicia's coldness towards her as my child withdraws. They take her to a child psychologist to try to find the little girl who smiled at them behind bars. And for every moment I feel the pain of Felicia's loss, I have to accept that Melanie feels it too. In her mind, the girl who's come home with her left her little soul in prison.

When Felicia leaves, it's like the click of a stopwatch that counts down to the day, the very hour, when I'll leave here. She's a magnet, drawing me from thousands of miles away. And although I'm sad at first, this injects a new energy into me. Bond, my lawyer, and I spend hours poring over pardons, amnesties, parole, reviews, appeals, to see which one will get me out of here as soon as possible. The only remaining option is a royal pardon. So in 1999, five years after I've been jailed and two years after Felicia has left, I submit an application for pardon to the King of Thailand.

The pardon consists of many documents that have to be sent from home. It's based on written submissions from my family members, including my mother, my sister, Melissa, and my brother, Marlon. A number of highly influential South Africans, including Anglican Archbishop Desmond Tutu, a respected anti-apartheid cleric, adds his voice to my family's appeals. They beg the King for mercy, saying I made a terrible mistake as a young woman and I'm a first-time offender with a young child who's been separated from me. They plead for me to be released on humanitarian grounds.

It bothers me that I have to plead guilty in this pardon. Why should I be forced to lie about the way it happened? Why should my family be forced to say I'm a drug-trafficker? But I soon learn there can be no mention of the truth in this pardon application. Bond reminds me that I could lose my child over a matter of pride. To deny guilt in a pardon that goes before the king would be to make a mockery of him and Thailand's justice system. Bond says this pardon is the one thing that could save my life.

Royal pardons are costly. First the documents have to be translated into Royal Thai, which differs significantly from the Thai written and spoken by ordinary people. This will have to be done by a Thai lawyer that Mrs Holmes has found me and it'll cost 15 000 baht, the equivalent of R2 500. This is a huge amount of money that would take me decades to earn in prison. But the same South African Airways hostess, who's brought me clothing and food previously, says she'll sponsor my application. I'm overjoyed! I know the King will be moved by words of such deep sincerity. And it won't be long before this pardon is granted and I can firmly shut Lard Yao out of my mind.

But I have to learn to be patient. It takes at least three full years for a pardon to go before the king for consideration. There's also no fixed date by when I'll have a response. But it still floods me with anticipation. I find a job at the computer company, Nettech, which has an office in Lard Yao. Over the course of eight years, I've managed to get a good grip of the Thai language and I spend many hours at the computer translating and proofreading documents and doing data capturing. I excel at this job. I'm also an assistant instructor in the thai chi and yoga classes held at the prison. It's all good preparation for when I leave Lard Yao.

As I enter my third year of waiting, hope bubbles inside me hard. Collette, who studied law and has been moving up in the legal ranks, has been fighting hard for me. And Paul Connell, formerly my neighbour when I lived in Berea, has been writing letters furiously to high-profile people on my behalf, asking them to approach the Thai King to ask for my release. Bond's waged his own campaign for my freedom in the South African press and by going to see influential politicians in person. When he visits me or writes to me, he tells me all about his experiences at the Union Buildings in Pretoria, the seat of our government.

He's never discouraged, even though he's seen a radical shift since Nelson Mandela's presidential term ended. During this time, Bond was convinced South Africa was so close to signing a treaty with Thailand to bring its prisoners back home. But he tells me that since the Thabo Mbeki administration has taken over, there's been a hardening of the government's viewpoint on this issue. One senior Foreign Affairs official says to Bond, "If you commit the crime there, you serve the time there."

For years, the Nigerian prisoners have suffered the most discrimination at Lard Yao. Many of them are charcoal-skinned and the Thais always favour light skin over dark. They call the Nigerians *kwai,* meaning buffalo. This leads to terrible fights between Thai and Nigerian inmates in which they use hand-carved knives and metal buckets as weapons. I see racism at its most raw in how the Nigerians are punished, how they're spoken to, how they're looked down upon. But just two years after the Nigerians begin complaining about their difficulties in jail, their government sets up an embassy in Bangkok.

And the day comes when Lard Yao's gates swing wide open and out of police vehicles pour Nigerian special forces, head to toe in black. They line the corridors, hard-faced as black slate, while the puny Thai officers shiver in their boots. They find 55 of their citizens serving time for all kinds of offences. And they dress them in beautiful West African prints, elegant headdresses. The national dress of their country. Those women shed their shame with their prison uniforms. Their pride and dignity restored in that small act. When I watch them go, I cry. I cry for the rest of us Africans stuck here. I know South Africa would never do the same – not even for the innocent among us.

That's why I've had to turn to the Thai King for mercy. I'm still a believer in miracles and sometimes, when I pass the prison gates, I picture myself walking through them without looking back, just like Felicia did. I can only be positive when I think of how it's all fallen into place – my air hostess friend coming to my rescue with all that money, Bond giving of his time and skills free of charge, a man like Desmond Tutu putting his name to my application. And I begin to plan ahead.

It won't be easy going back to South Africa after spending this long at Lard Yao. But I'm only thirty years old. There's still time for me to start a new life from scratch and I'm not too old to revive dreams that I've been nursing for such a long time. I imagine how I'll have to re-introduce myself to Felicia slowly, especially now that she's accepted Melanie as her mom over the last eight years. And I'll finally be able to stay true to my promise that I'll be home soon – even if soon hasn't been as short a time as my child expected. I share all these expectations with the two women who've become especially close to me lately, La Tasha Madson and Kairit Aron. When I'm not feeling as strong as I should be, they give me courage and remind me that my time here could be over any day now.

In December 2001, just over three years since I've submitted my pardon, I'm called into the office. I think nothing of it – they routinely called us in. But when I'm asked to sit across from the officer seated there, I wonder why this meeting's suddenly become so formal. She's even laid out a pink tablecloth on a table that's always bare.

"Your pardon come back," she says lightly.

I feel my heart thump! I'm so thrilled! I lean forward towards her as she breaks this news to me – this news that will change my life. Eight years of suffering, of waiting, of injustice, are about to end right now! I almost want to cry already, I'm so grateful this day's come...

"They reject it, Wanessa."

I'm stung. "What? No, no. That can't be right," I say. "Read it again. Please. Please read it again..."

She looks down at her piece of paper. Plants a firm finger under the line.

"It say here, Wanessa. Pardon rejected."

"But why? Why?" My voice has suddenly become so loud, so desperate.

She flinches, then says in a low voice, "Because you a drug case..."

"Not even... not even a reduction of sentence...?"

"No, Wanessa, nothing."

I stand up to go.

"You apply again after two years?" she asks, almost cheerfully. What is it with these Thais who think a smile fits every occasion? They wear the same expression to weddings as to funerals. And right now, I hate it. I want to punch this smile off her face. Does she understand the seriousness of what she's just said to me?

Before she called me in here, did she even take a moment to count the years? My years! My lost years! All the time I should've spent raising my child and getting married and growing my business and studying and working and buying a house and a car and a dog! All the time that's passed, all the seconds and minutes and days and weeks and months and years I've survived in this hellhole on this lie called hope! I'm an idiot! How could I turn this into such a crutch? I'm a fool. My throat closes. I can't answer her. I don't know that I'll even survive two more years in this stinking place. I can't even see as far ahead as the next minute, and she wants me to decide if I'll apply in two years – what for? Just so their King can say no to me again?

I turn around and leave, barefoot, my shoes abandoned there, under the table. But I don't go back for them. I don't care anymore.

Lard Yao sees, controls, owns everything here, including the lives of all the people who come here. I rush out into the day. I want it to burn me, this sunlight that's been so blistering hot since I woke up. Now, it's beating down on my bare arms and face. And I know it should feel like walking through a furnace. I want it to scorch me! But I feel nothing. I look down at the heat steaming off the ground that should feel like a hot iron under my feet. But it doesn't. I should cry. I want to cry. I know I should cry. I close my eyes and clench them. Try to force the tears out. But my ducts are stinging, as though they've dried up.

All I feel is the bitter disappointment sitting in the depths of me like a cold, hard stone I've swallowed. And then, a slow numbness begins to flow through me. Like mercury in my veins. Thick and cold. I feel like she's just handed me a death sentence. And I'm suddenly saying aloud to myself again and again: "There's no way out. There's no way out. You're never going to get out of here! There's no way out."

A switch is flicked somewhere. It plunges me into a dense, malty darkness, a syrupy black tar churning at the very centre of me. My heart closes. My mind shuts down. Only my body will keep going – for now. I sit somewhere. And I think and think until the hope's bled out of me and I'm sitting in the wetness of it. And I suddenly realise, it's not these people or their prison or their country or their justice system I hate.

It's me.

"It's you, Vanessa," I whisper. *"I hate you."*

CHAPTER 18

Sinking

Vanessa is dead.

That weak, pathetic Vanessa, who cried, who pleaded, who clung to the truth of her innocence, who believed in the core goodness of people. She's dead. I killed her. And I'm all that remains. I had to do it, because no cotton-wool-lined woman can survive in a place like this. The women who come to Lard Yao are like trees that have to sacrifice branches in drought and times of hardship. Part of them must die, so the rest of them can live.

It happens the day I find out about the failed pardon. The day that meek Vanessa, who used to be me, goes to the office like a calf to a slaughterhouse. A calf that should know its awful fate lies just a few steps ahead because it can smell the blood of others in front of it. But it goes with such eagerness anyway. That was just stupid, believing a miracle could happen. And that was what killed naïve, gullible Vanessa. But now that she's dead and buried in this prison, I can go on. No one will look for her or find her because everyone knows Lard Yao swallows human beings. Either we leave here alive and without a soul, or pass through those gates in a body bag.

But honestly, I feel freer somehow – wiped clean of that childish faith and innocence that used to be a part of me. That forced me to live some impossible dream of returning home for so long.

These days, I see myself reflected in the concrete of Lard Yao. A stoniness in my face, a bitterness at the back of my throat like the brown, rusty water that drips from these decaying pipes. My blood feels dark and thick. And I have a lightning-bolt moment in which I realise I deserve to be here. I deserve to be punished. Because I'm the cause of all of this. I'm the reason my mother tried to kill herself more than once. I'm the reason my daughter is sitting halfway across the world with a broken heart.

This is all I think of every day for hours. And the thought sharpens, grows into a blade. A long, thick silver shaft that jackhammers through my brain, drills into me, makes me desperate and frenzied. Reminds me all the time of how I'm failing those I love. It maddens me, makes me tremble with anger, with shame. And when it rattles me, makes me shake like that, I'm suddenly driven to do such insane things. I pretend I'm no longer human. Each moment I spend in this body, I play a cruel game with it. I see how far I can push it. Every limb, every muscle, every organ. Pushed a little harder every day. Tested to the very limits that it'll go.

I won't rest. Resting is weakness. I'm up before the sky breaks open. I fly into the Nettech offices as they open, talk to no one, spend hours proofreading, translating, re-reading, translating, back-translating paragraphs, pages, reams, entire libraries that tumble on top of me. But I lie buried beneath them, still going at a furious pace. I never stop for anything. Not to drink. Not to eat. Not to breathe. Machine-like, robotic, my fingers drum hard all day on that keyboard, my wrists aching from the thousands of words that multiply like viruses on the screen. My eyes are gritty. They are failing, but I will not look away until I've lunged into the next task.

There are no breaks for me. I blur past the others pushing, elbowing, lining up for their lunch. I no longer need food to get by. I rip my prison uniform off, pull on my gym clothes and teach hours of aerobics, sprinting between buildings to give the next class and the next class and another class. They all pass in a dizzying whirl of sweat and breathlessness. I shower, I dash back to work.

To glue myself to my chair, to lock my eyes onto the screen. To bind my fingers back to that keyboard. Tap tap tap. Tap tap tap. And the blankness of that screen is suddenly filled with a colony of words crawling like ants.

And when everyone is streaming back to their cells for the night, I'll enter mine with piles of files in my arms so I can hardly see anything in front of me. These are the deadlines I set for myself, bullying myself, sitting cramped on the concrete floors into the early hours of the morning: proofreading, translating, translating, proofreading, chains of words warping, snakelike, around me, squeezing verbs and nouns and adjectives and full stops and question marks out of me until I can hardly breathe anymore.

And at sun up, I'm exercising, teaching this body a lesson – this body that bore an innocent baby that I sent away. That I shipped off like an animal in a crate. I don't eat. I don't sleep. There's no time for these luxuries anymore. And my friends. What's wrong with them? Why won't they shut up? They're always in my ear, whispering, shouting, "Vanessa, you're too thin! Vanessa, you're too skinny! What's wrong? Talk to us." I don't want to talk to you. I don't want to talk to anyone. Don't you understand? We talk and talk but our words mean nothing. They're puffs of stale air that do nothing to change our situation. We're stuck here so shut up! I don't want to hear what you have to say.

And at night, a frantic nervousness sets in. My heart is a pump on steroids, beating so hard, so fast, slamming into my organs, hammering against my ribs. I lie panting, even when I'm dead still. I look down and my body's suddenly wasted away, shrunken inwards, my skin vacuum-sealed over my bones. I tie my skirt roughly, tightly, so it won't slip down my bony hips. It's so tight that it leaves marks on me. My face is sharp, gaunt. And suddenly, I'm terrified! At night when I start nodding off and feel sleep slithering at my feet, I wake myself up in a panic. Don't sleep, Vanessa! It'll crush you! What if you never wake up? You'll die in your sleep if you close your eyes. Don't sleep. Whatever you do, don't sleep! Death will creep in here and suffocate you!

This thought haunts me every night. Robs me of every moment

I could shut these eyes to stop the feeling of jagged rocks under my eyelids, scratching at my eyeballs, grazing them, tearing them apart. And in the morning when I take that first sip of water, the smell and taste of blood swamp my nose and mouth, a metallic slick all over my tongue that makes me want to vomit.

Something's wrong with me. I don't know what. All I know is, there's something wrong. I burst into Lard Yao's hospital room.

"I need help! There's something wrong with me! My heart beats so fast. It races all day and all night. I can't sleep. I haven't slept for weeks. What's wrong with me?"

And the nurse is just standing there, looking at me strangely, asking me to have a blood test. She jabs my raised blue vein. "We call you if test positive," is all she says.

I stumble out of there and go back to the high-speed treadmill of my life. All peaks, no valleys. But no one calls back from the hospital. Why not? Why haven't they called me back? There's something wrong! Can't anyone see? I'm banging on her door again. Banging hard, watching my pounding knuckles go white against the wooden door. "Why you come back? Nothing wrong! Blood test say you HIV negative. While you walking you still fine!" she says. But I'm not walking. I'm running and I'm staggering. I'm tripping and falling over myself. I'm exhausted. So exhausted. And my friends, I've pushed them away, kicked at them so hard, they say they don't know me anymore. I laugh mockingly at them. How can they know me when I'm a stranger even to myself right now?

And then one day it happens. It grabs me while I'm jumping over all those high hurdles and I suddenly can't breathe. My chest is closed. I'm hunched over, trying to force the thinnest stream of air into my lungs. But it goes into my mouth and stays trapped there. It won't go any further, even though my lungs are straining for it. And there's an invisible pair of hands clamped around my throat, crushing, squeezing, tightening, choking, strangling me. I'm gasping, I'm shuddering. The blood is draining out of my feet. Then out of my hands. They're so chilled. I'm sweating and shivering at the same time. And there's a massive boulder being lifted and smashed against my head again and again. My skull's being crushed. And I'm bashing on the doctor's door. Saying, help me! Something is wrong. I know something is wrong! But he turns around and says, "No, you're fine."

So I run out to this life again and I keep it going, the fast-forward juggling of these fire sticks, so afraid I will drop them and set myself alight. And one day I'm in the shower, icy water coursing over me, goose flesh rising like nettles from my skin and I instantly feel it again. That swaying in my knees and the vibration in my chest, so hard, that when I look down it seems my heart's shifted and leapt forward to the very edge of my skin. And it's battering it, smashing against it so fast, so hard, that there's a greying of the picture in front of me, a child's hands scribbling, colouring it black, in large, wide strokes, until the pitch black paint falls over and floods the whole picture, smothering all the gaps. And the floor begins racing towards me at a terrifying speed. There's nothing I can do to stop it from crashing into me.

I wake up on a bench just in front of Lard Yao hospital. My eyes snap open, and I can see the shadow of figures overhead, dashing around me. Voices as distorted as if we're underwater. And then I see the bag of smelling salts the nurse has held under my nose to bring me to. But when I try to move, when I try to talk, nothing happens. I can't open my mouth, can't coax any words out. My arms, my legs, my mouth, my entire body. Loose, drooling, drooping, sagging, slumping, spent. Ragdoll tired.

Now there's shouting. I lie there and hear La Tasha arguing with the nurse. La Tasha says she's not doing enough to help me. Is that fear I hear in La Tasha's voice? She's screaming at the nurse now. "I'll call the embassy to tell them how you're treating Vanessa!" I want to say something – tell La Tasha to calm down, but I'm sand-throated and thick-tongued. And this nurse has had enough of La Tasha's insults. She wants to shut the door in her face. There's a pounding of footsteps. The prison director is here. She wants me rushed upstairs and admitted to hospital right now. But how will I get there? I can't move! I'm a dead weight they grab on both sides and drag up the stairs, my feet two floppy fins trailing behind me. They heave me onto a creaky bed, my body splashed there, my limbs hanging over the sides. They grab my limp hand, find a vein, puncture it and stick a drip into me.

I'm so frightened that I may be paralysed. I have to test each part of me – see which is working and which is not. So I mentally call to each of them to see if they're still connected to me and alive. I can feel them. I can feel them all. But I can't move them, like concrete's been poured thick all around me and I'm set in it. I close my eyes. Focus my mind hard. If I could just find one burst of strength – just one last spark of energy that's lying buried somewhere in me – I would lift my arm, I would open my mouth, I would say just one word. I try. I try so many times. I try so hard. But I can't. There's a fatigue, a weariness inside me so deep, so heavy, I can feel it shimmering in the marrow of my bones, radiating outwards through the strained fibres of my muscles that lie like torn frayed bits of rope under my skin. It'll pass, I tell myself. I have to believe it'll pass.

But this single moment, in which I feel such complete helplessness, grows and expands, first into days, then into weeks and into months. It feels terminal, hospice-like. A countdown to dying. A young woman at the hospital called Tang Moo does everything for me. She feeds me, she cleans me, she washes my clothes, she allows me to fling my scrawny frame at her as she hauls me to the toilet. And she does it all in exchange for a few meals that I receive from friends and the head of the prison every day – food that will go to waste, because I can hardly manage a mouthful.

Me Chook, the prison head is especially kind to me. She gives the hospital staff strict orders to take good care of me. She sends me water-rice, an egg or a piece of chicken every day and she comes round to check on how I'm doing each evening. Night after night, she walks away disappointed at how little progress I've made. But in the days that I'm lying there, shut away to everyone but myself, there are many things that reveal themselves to me. This exhaustion that's eaten into me like a parasite – it didn't just choose me as a host because of how I've strained my body. My mind is worn out too, all its defences fallen over. And most of all, my spirit's been defeated.

I've spent all this time battling the system. Eight years of fighting for a place to sleep, a place in a line so I can queue for food, eight years of fighting for hot water, hanging space, a place to sit. Fighting to prove my innocence, but in the end being forced to plead guilty. Fighting to keep my child and losing her. Fighting for my freedom and being told I don't deserve to have it. Despair stabs me like a knife in the breastbone, inserts itself into me, says *I've come to live here*. This pain is too hard to bear. I can't take it anymore. I don't know how to go on without knowing when I'll see my mother or my child again.

My friends come to the hospital to visit me regularly. But the way they look at me unnerves me. There's pity. There's fear in their eyes. I wish I could see exactly what they see. They sit at my bedside and try to talk to me, try to make sense of the wild, rambling thoughts falling like chewed rice out of the corners of my mouth. I think they're worried I'll die. And so what if I do? All I can think these days is that there's such salvation in death and all I'm yearning for is that peace.

CHAPTER 19

The depths below

I lie there for days, a bag of juice the colour of plasma plugged into my vein, dribbling into me like embalming fluid. In this hospital, I get no answers as to what's actually wrong with me. The absence of doctors means the nurses are expected to make medical decisions they're not qualified to. La Tasha and Kairit take messages on my behalf to their visitors, asking them to please contact the South African embassy because I'm seriously ill. Many of them do. But for a long time, there's still no word from the new embassy counsellor until one day I'm called to the embassy room for a visit. I shouldn't go because my body's refusing. But I can't snub an embassy official. I also need the embassy to write a letter to Thailand's Ministry of Correctional Services, asking for permission for me to be moved to a proper hospital.

Two young women help me out of my bed and almost carry me to the embassy room because I'm still unable to walk. I sprawl into a chair, hardly able to support my own head. The counsellor sits opposite me, a snarl on her face.

"Why did you get so many people to call me to come?"

She's angry, but I'm in no position to fight back. I try to whisper something back to her but my reedy voice won't travel beyond the wire mesh to the other side.

"You know how busy I am?"

She's sitting here belittling me because I can't match her strength or aggression. Khun Patchala Porn is the high-ranking officer on duty. She's watching this meeting. And it doesn't take her long to step in.

"How can you speak to her like that? Vanessa is sick. Can't you see that?"

"Ja, but why does she have to get so many people to call me?"

"What do you expect? She can't call. She's got no phone. That's why she asked someone to call you!"

The counsellor snorts a response I can't hear. She lacks the sensitivity this job requires. I turn to Khun Patchala Porn and ask her to come closer. I manage to rasp: "Tell this woman... I don't want... to see her anymore." The officer gives her the message and the counsellor leaves in a huff.

Weeks later, Lard Yao's nurses contact the embassy again to ask for the letter I need to visit another hospital. Surprisingly, the embassy approves it. The prison director signs it and I'm allowed to go to Klong Prem Hospital next door. Dr Panapong, the long-haired hippie doctor is in charge. He runs a number of tests, does X-rays on me and I return to Lard Yao to wait for the results. But when they're due, Dr Panapong is on leave and I'm sent to Dr One Eye, the groper, for him to interpret the results. It's been hard enough for me to come here. But now I have to sit opposite him, holding my body up while he sifts through a pile of result sheets to figure out which one is mine. He looks at my results and nods his head.

"You HIV positive", he says.

"What..? No... That can't be..."

I'm horrified! This can't be possible. I muster the last bit of strength I have and reach across the table to grab the card out of his hand. My eye immediately falls on the patient's name.

"This is not my card," I say as firmly as I can, although it comes out more like a murmur. He takes it back and has a good look.

"No, these not your results. They for someone else."

I get up and hobble out with help. I can't sit here in this room with him a minute longer and he's upset with me for making him

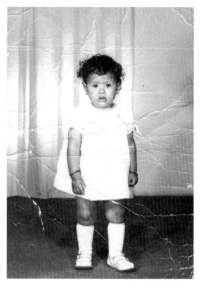

Vanessa at 1 year and 8 months

Vanessa, Collette, Christine and Melanie during their high-school days

Vanessa, Melanie, Christine and Collette in high school – friends forever

Vanessa's modelling continued after school at fashion shows

Rushda Dolley – Vanessa's aunt and foster mother

Minah Goosen – Vanessa's mother at 63 years old

Vanessa in a garment designed by Glenn Duvall Pettway from Chicago

Vanessa in police van

Vanessa and Felicia are given milk formula to pose with in the dining hall at the gong li un

Vanessa and Felicia get called to the gong li un *to take pictures; it was also an opportunity to get something nice to eat*

Vanessa with Felicia at 1 month and 16 days

Felicia sitting on an officer's bed, crying and afraid of the cameraman – pictures taken to be sent home had to paint the prison in a positive light

Vanessa and Felicia in the visiting room – picture taken by a South African visitor

Vanessa with Felicia at 2 years and 5 months – the annual picture taken by the authorities which was allowed to be sent home

Lard Yao Central Women's Correctional Institution in Bangkok, Thailand

*Me Wee –
Felicia's Thai
prison mother*

*Vanessa's prison ID card
with death commuted to a life
sentence*

*Vanessa teaching aerobics in
prison to over 5 000 inmates on
the King's birthday*

*Vanessa with Michael and Rachel McCarthy while Vanessa was part of
the prison choir – photo taken outside the prison*

Vanessa modelling garments designed and manufactured inside Lard Yao – the fashion show was held outside the prison with guards in attendance

Vanessa modelling outside the prison in clothes designed by prisoners

Felicia, Melanie and Lerell on the day that Felicia left Thailand – her third birthday

A letter to Felicia from Vanessa – Felicia was too young to read or write so this was how they communicated

Felicia with her foster family – Hilton, Melanie and Lerell Holmes

Felicia with Father Christmas at 9 years old

Mpumelelo Nyoka, aka 'Bond', with Vanessa's sister Melissa

The late Thobile Boltina, former president Thabo Mbeki and Bond in 1998, a year after handing over Vanessa's plea request

Markus Gyssler from Germany   *Per from Norway*

Vanessa's sister Jacky Goosen, who passed away just before her release in 2010

Eileen with Mrs Holmes' prison ministry team at the airport to say goodbye to Vanessa

Vanessa saying goodbye at the Bangkok airport

Vanessa and Eileen Boelkas at the Bangkok airport

Lourdes and Charles Holmes with Vanessa at the Bangkok airport

Vanessa back on South African soil, on the beach in Port Elizabeth

Vanessa and Collette – reunited after 16 years and 6 months

Hilton and Felicia at 16 years old

Pastor Pretorius and Collette Holmes at the airport waiting for Vanessa's arrival in South Africa

Vanessa's first pool party for her birthday in 2010 at Elmarie's house

*Vanessa and Felicia at Felicia's Matric
Farewell in 2012*

*Vanessa's first shopping experience after her release – she spent three
hours in the store browsing*

Dr Marlin McKay and Vanessa

Vanessa and Rachel McCarthy – Vanessa's spiritual mother – on her visit to South Africa

Vanessa at a motivational talk for ACSA, OR Tambo International Airport, 2011

Markus and Vanessa at her welcoming party

Vanessa with her great aunt – Aunty Suze – pictured here at 84 – her prayer was to remain alive just to see Vanessa again

Vanessa Goosen – picture by Naomi Estment

look like a fool. At some stage of my illness, he also prescribes antibiotics for me, even though my prison card clearly says I'm allergic to penicillin.

I go back to Lard Yao where I wait for Dr Panapong to come back because One-Eye's too offended to read me the correct results. A few days later, Dr Panapong comes to Lard Yao, sits me down and explains that I've been suffering from anxiety. He says I need Hepatitis A, B and C injections, which I have to pay for. He also says I've been having panic attacks and they can be very dangerous.

"You could've had a heart attack, Vanessa," he says in fluent English. "You have to calm down and take things easy. You're also suffering from depression."

Even though he gives the nurses permission to discharge me, one of them knows I'm still quite frail, so she lets me stay at the hospital a little longer.

There's a lady in the bed next to me who's suffering from high blood pressure. One day she eats a fruit that's high in cholesterol and suddenly gets violently ill. Minutes later, she's dead. The nurses can't be bothered to try to save her. For starters, she's just another inmate. But there's also such a deep belief in reincarnation among Thais that death doesn't bother them. In their eyes, she's just passed from one state of being into another. The nurses go about their duties as if she was never there to begin with.

But it plays on my mind for hours. I think of the finality that marks this tussle of life and death, both pulling their own way until life finally gives in. And as this woman's body lies there, cooling from this battle she's finally lost, I think of what thoughts went through her head and how brave she must've been to face those last moments without the slightest bit of love or compassion. What courage it takes to fight when you're alone. And I'm terrified by this thought – it was this woman's turn today but it could just as well have been me, dying alone, no one who loves me by my side, bound to this bed, thousands of kilometres away from home. And I suddenly feel that this wasn't a mere coincidence, but an omen, a prediction of how my own life is going to end. Not a word to my daughter or my mother. No goodbye to my friends. But if this is how my life will end, I decide then and there that I won't put up a fight. I've fought for long enough. From now on, whatever happens will happen.

They don't bother taking my neighbour's body away that day. It saddens me that I didn't know her name. Night comes and she's lying there next to me in all her eerie stillness, her orifices plugged to stop her death juices from flowing out, a thick halo of powder sprinkled round her bed to keep the ants away. Her shape pokes through the sheet that covers her. I can trace the curves of her face, her chest, her arms and legs through that sheet. A body just like mine, missing only the breath of life, a line as thin as a communion wafer separating the living and the dead.

These thoughts make me so anxious, so upset, that I begin gasping for air until the nurses run in and clamp an oxygen mask over my face. All I want is for them to take this body away. I can't look at it anymore. I can't imagine surviving a whole night with this corpse lying next to me. They ignore me. After a while, calm comes over me. I walk over to her corpse. I pull the sheet over her icy feet, sticking out, and tuck it underneath them. She deserves just a little bit of dignity.

A team arrives the next day. They throw her into an orange body bag and carry her away as if it were the most normal thing to leave her in that bed, rotting in Bangkok's heat overnight. But I become obsessed with the idea of death. With how close it's brushed against me, sinister as a cat, as if it wanted to take me too. And that smell never leaves my nostrils. The smell of desperation that comes with dying alone. Of organs leaking their last fluids. The staleness of old meat that grips the air, tissue liquefying, sickly sweet. All the things that used to be hidden from me behind the walls of mortuaries. They have come and presented themselves here and reminded me that everything I've seen happen to her will happen to me too.

I'm traumatised by this. By these lingering thoughts of death that will never leave me alone. They especially haunt me at night when I turn to her empty bed and see her there again, a ghostly outline in her crumpled sheet, calling to me. One anxiety attack after the other hits me. They pin me down, they knife me. I scream and gasp and cry and choke, and then it's suddenly over, until the next one erupts. Every bit of progress I've made since coming here has been undone.

Slowly, willingly, I relapse into that state of inaction. My body becomes a splatter on the bed. And when I lie here with everything shut down, there's at least a feeling of calm in the blackness. The silence under my eyelids is comforting and tranquil, like the cool, dark inside of a coffin. I feel myself drifting and I know I might as well let myself be carried off. There's no Felicia. There's little chance I'll survive this to see my family or my country again. My spirit is broken. My body doesn't want to hold me anymore.

I've been in this state for weeks when the foreigner finds me. She's walked past, glimpsed me through the open door. She knows my story. That's why she's here today. She stands at the foot of my bed. She touches my feet.

"Vanessa, you're ice cold…" she says. And I know what she's thinking. That I'm already dead from the waist down. And that's when she begins to say these things to me.

"Vanessa, you can't do this. You're a very selfish person. How can you think about yourself first? You don't think about your daughter. You don't think about your family." And as she says this, she grabs my feet and starts praying for me.

I want to fight it. I want to fight her. Not just for calling me selfish, but for these empty words pouring from her mouth, talking to a God I know won't listen to her. I know, because I've begged him and he's ignored me. He's left me here to die without my child. But suddenly, this woman is invoking him. She's asking him to come to this room, to come to me and save me from dying alone here. She's begging him to spare me so I can see my daughter again one day, and when Felicia's name falls from her lips, that face, my child's exquisite face, floods my mind. The face I've blotted out for months because it hurts too much to look at it. But it's here now, hovering in front of me and instantly it's real to me again. I can touch it. I can run my fingers over it. Feel her soft child skin. Trace the smile that hides her pain at being born into such an unfair world.

I'm her mother. I'm the woman who travelled in excruciating pain to King's Hospital to bring my child into the world. I nursed her and cared for her and protected her and gave her to the one woman I knew would love Felicia as her own. But I have never stopped loving my child. Never stopped yearning for her. I yearn for her still, now. And that's why I can't die! I can't die without seeing her. After making her this promise that I'll be back soon, I can't abandon her by breaking it. She doesn't deserve it. Felicia's enough to live for. She's saved me from the firing squad and now, still, the promise of seeing her again, of being a real mother to her one day, is keeping me alive even though she's so far away. In my mind, I whisper, *I won't leave you, Felicia. I'll never leave you. I'll fight to stay alive! I'll fight to come home, no matter how long it takes...*

And suddenly there's the cool trickling of something inside me, like the sound of spring water between rocks. It's bubbling, welling up. It stirs at the centre of my being and suddenly surges upwards in one massive current, through my stomach, up my throat, forcing my mouth open. And I let it out. An ear-splitting cry that charges every dying cell in me to life. I lie there and I cry. I weep for Felicia, for my lost years behind bars, for my mother who's tried to end her own life because I lost mine, for my sisters who've gone without my love for the past eight years. I sob for Vanessa. For that young woman who believed and had faith and was so trusting and grew up believing the world was a good place, full of decent people. I want to bring her back! I want to draw her remains out of every brick of every wall of Lard Yao she's buried in. I want to infuse myself with her again. I want to be that woman who would never give up on anything, especially her child. So I say aloud, because I know she'll come if she hears it, "I don't want to die!" I say it again and again until I'm sure she hears me. *"I don't want to die! Can you hear me? I said, I don't want to die!"*

And then I feel it, a slow, gentle warmth, tingling at my toes. Like they're dangling over the edge of a warm bath. The flame spreads slowly, warms my feet. It streams upwards into my ankles, my legs, my thighs, my core, my heart, my head. Thaws me to the bone. And when I open my eyes again, I suddenly know I've been saved. Pulled from the brink. I'm still afraid, but it's a different kind of fear. I'm afraid of dying because I came so close, and life has suddenly become so precious to me again.

And from that day on, I fight like a militant to stay alive. When I struggle to eat, I roll the bread into a ball, shove it down my throat and chase it down with water. I try to teach myself to live again, never to surrender until I know it really is my time to die. It's a few days before I get up from that bed. I can see outside the hospital windows and each time I look out there, I motivate myself to push hard till I'm out there again. I force myself out of bed. I'm so weak, I almost collapse. But everyone seems so willing to help me. I take only two steps a day at first. My goals are small, but rewarding. I add two steps onto the total number I take every day. And one day, after trying for so long, I reach the door. I'm over the moon! I look at the bed and see my impression there, in the sheets. And it thrills me to think I've made it off my deathbed.

☾

Melanie gives me the best gift she ever could. Almost two years into my recovery, she brings Felicia back for the second time to Lard Yao to see me. My body is still sore from the beating it's taken, and when I take my place in that seat in the embassy room, I feel every part of me groan. But then I look up and she's there. Felicia with her angelic nine-year-old face. I'm amazed at how she's grown. She's tall and slightly plump, but she still has this little baby face, framed by long hair. There's a cute smile on her face and she doesn't stop talking, bombarding me with questions: Why are you so skinny and why have you got a pimple and why's your hair grey and what are you doing inside? And for a moment I feel completely normal. Just an ordinary mom with her extraordinary kid, talking about the boring stuff that life's made of.

"My friends ask me about you," she says. "What should I tell them if they ask?"

"Don't tell them where your mother is," I say, "because if you tell them, they'll make fun of you. They'll tease you. I don't want that, so don't tell them I'm in prison, okay?"

"I won't tell them you're in prison, Mommy – I'll tell them you're in jail…"

I smile at her innocence.

"That's the same thing, my baby. You can't tell them that. When they ask, tell them I'm working in Bangkok in Thailand for an IT company."

It's a half-truth, but not a complete lie.

I look at this little girl who's only four years away from teenage-hood now and think back to her visit with me in prison at the age of five – the first time she came back after leaving Lard Yao. And I remember the anger in her eyes towards Melanie, but especially me. She didn't call me Mommy. She only turned to Hilton and said, "I don't want to see *her*. I don't want to speak to *her*!" That visit devastated me. And yet now, here she is – older and more forgiving, able to understand this situation a bit better. I laugh with her, we share stories of our separate lives and try to figure out how they meet somewhere in the middle.

A few weeks after they get back, Melanie writes to me to say Felicia's been telling her friends all about me.

"My mommy lives in a big house in Thailand, with a big garden. My mom's as tall as the roof and she works with computers."

Melanie's amused at how my version of the story has grown into this tall tale that Felicia's friends all find so impressive. I'm emotional. My child hasn't forgotten me. And even though I carry the shame of being in prison, she's not ashamed of me.

I'm still larger than life, someone special who lives a happy life in a pleasant place. That's what I let her believe. I don't want her to know how hard life can get in here. But one day, when I leave this place, I'll tell her about the time I almost died and how she gave me the strength to fight, the courage to stay alive. My time at Lard Yao may run into many more years, but now I can face them, because I know for sure Felicia has never stopped loving me, just as I've loved her a little more each day that I have lost with her while in this prison.

CHAPTER 20

Finding purpose

I've lost four years of my life to depression. The day I lay on that bed crawling towards the end and I chose to turn back and fight, was the day I started clawing my way back to life. I'm not sure if Yard Lao can be called life. It was all that lay outside of that hospital room for me and I had no other choice but to take it. But I've learnt in the last few years that the journey back to "normality" is never easy.

Once you've slipped into that inky pool of sadness and hopelessness, once you've swum with your head below the surface, you never quite forget the taste and feel of it, the roots below that wrap around you to suffocate you, the slime that coats your skin. And when you climb out of it, it's not long before you realise you've forgotten what life is like on the outside.

My body will never let me forget that I was once in that hospital fighting for my sanity and my life. My body has a mind of its own. And it's so used to overreacting, so used to living off anxiety, that this is all it wants to do even after I'm discharged. That's when the fighting really begins. When I'm trying to steer myself back to the old Vanessa – the one who was mostly in control – and my body simply refuses.

It batters me with fear. It shuts down my lungs so I can't breathe. It sends flames shooting through my body in hot flushes. It makes me choke from imagining those invisible hands clamped around my throat. My body wants me to give into failure. To collapse, as though it needs those short moments of peace between the rat race. For a year and a half after I leave the hospital, this is the constant battle raging between my body and mind.

I faint all the time. I wake up and carry on until I faint again. My body doesn't seem to remember being strong and able. It recalls only this limpness, like a fish that's just been caught and wriggles and fights for half a minute before its eyes go dead. My friends are drained. They've supported me, but I'm still not myself. I walk short distances, then have to rest. I need help showering and dressing. I'm still not sleeping. And my menstrual cycle is suddenly two weeks of cruel cramping, knives in my back and stomach.

The husband-and-wife missionary team who've been writing to me, Rachel and Michael, send me some information about depression and anxiety from the internet. And only then do I realise that it's possible to die, not just from injury to the body, but from injury to the mind and spirit too. I'm sent to the prison psychologist. She understands me and reassures me that the condition I have is the result of the trauma I've experienced over many years now. And I'm not the only one suffering from these kinds of attacks. I suddenly realise I'm not a freak.

She insists I start taking anti-depressants and prescribes me a tablet that's non-addictive and has no side-effects. I hate taking medication but I need to do this to go forward with my life. So every night, I line up where the medicine is handed out and I'm given my pill. A contraceptive pill is soon added to this because of my painful periods.

But while the pills condition my body, I must condition my mind. I make it a point of returning to all the places I've developed a phobia about after fainting there. And I force myself to stand there and tell myself, as panicked as I am, that this is the only way to break the fear. I repeat to myself, "You have to break the fear, Vanessa." And I do. Ever so slowly.

I force myself to start resuming my responsibilities. I go back to work in the computer room, although my workload is much lighter than before. I also gradually start doing my daily aerobics.

But I need to feed my soul too. I need to reach out to other human beings in Lard Yao. I remember how I struggled to raise Felicia as a new mother in prison. And when I see these women pass me, their babies in their arms, I'm drawn to them.

There's a fear in their eyes from the shock of a prison childbirth. A weariness from the lack of sleep and a hopelessness that comes from not knowing what to do for this tiny human being. I take steps to help them – the pregnant women *and* the mothers, because that's what I would've wished for when I gave birth to Felicia here, eleven years ago. Many of them have just found out during their child's birth that they are HIV positive. Some of them already have TB.

These women are curious about Christianity and ask me to share what little I know about it. I know I'd never have survived the years in Lard Yao without my faith. And even when you realise human beings can do nothing more to help you, there's still one more place you can go for comfort.

I tell them the one thing I love about Jesus is that he was never some high-minded leader who sat apart from his suffering people. And maybe he knows how we feel because at the end, he's beaten and mocked and spat at as he walks through the streets carrying his cross. And he goes before Pontius Pilate, who knows that he's innocent but gives him the death sentence anyway. There's no way out for him and his humiliation is so public. He's not that Jesus of the neat white loin cloth. He's that Jesus who's stripped naked and flogged and has nails driven through him and has to die on the cross without one last shred of dignity while his broken-hearted mother looks on. And that's why I think he sees our pain and feels for every one of us trapped here.

I see the women for two short periods in the day – in the morning at about 7:15 and at lunchtime. I need special permission to meet them, since group meetings are usually not allowed for security reasons. So I ask the officers stationed outside the buildings to please allow me to visit the women there, to spend time with them twice a day. Permission is granted.

We read one Bible verse for the day, pray for strength to make it through the next twenty-four hours and, most importantly, they share their problems with me. Sometimes, they need emotional comfort, but at other times, they have problems that need solving. They may have run out of money and may be unable to feed their babies. Or their children may have reached the age of one year and need to be handed over to relatives on the outside.

Because I have no telephone access, Albert Blanc, an American missionary working with Mrs Holmes, helps me. He contacts the families of inmates, arranges for children to be fostered and provides help or medication to mothers and babies who are ill, but aren't getting the attention they need. If a mother is short of food or clothing for her child, I arrange this through the missionaries too.

Right now, I'm using my own money to buy milk, Cerelac and other necessities for the children. But my spiritual mother, Rachel, says, "You can't help like this, Vanessa. You've got to help with what you have." So I start a small organisation called The International Families' Support Group. It's formed to help the pregnant women, mothers and TB patients of Lard Yao prison. I also design a card which we sell. That money is deposited into an account handled by the missionaries.

Often, the women needing the most help are those leaving prison. The 500 baht we give them covers the cost of civilian clothes, their taxi fare to get home and some basics like milk formula and clothing for their children. Working with HIV-positive mothers opens my eyes to many things, especially the shame Thai society views these infected women with.

HIV/AIDS was once a game of skittles in this prison. This fast-moving disease rushing at young women, making them fall over in all directions. Every single day, without fail, we stood and watched them leave in body bags because there were no anti-retroviral drugs available. But that picture has changed quite a bit in the last few years. Many women now line up to be given these tablets that will save their lives.

There's a South African prisoner called Anna I met when I first came to Lard Yao. And lately she's been looking for friendship. In recent weeks, I've seen her go from being a well-built, large person to a stickwoman. One day, one of the nurses mentions to me, in passing, the results of Anna's blood test from a few months ago. "You not know she HIV positive?" she asks, surprised, because she's seen us together several times. "Test come back positive, but she no want take medication," she shrugs and casually moves on to doing something else. I'm not really surprised. All that weight Anna's lost in a matter of months. The constant diarrhoea she's been suffering from. I wish she'd told me. I could've organised some medication for her if she'd just asked.

I don't know how to broach the subject with her. There are times when she gets angry and lashes out and I don't want her to think I've gone behind her back to ask about her health. But it won't be long before her secret's out anyway. The prison officials soon realise that Anna's health has taken such a bad turn it's time they sent her to the tiny room where they send all their TB and HIV-positive patients. It's dark, dingy, filthy and crowded. Bodies line every centimetre of the floor. And in the middle, like a shrine, is a bed. One single bed. A bed no one wants to sleep on because whoever is promoted off the floor onto that bed knows their time is limited. Strapped into adult nappies, battling a body now completely out of their control, they lie there, slipping away, a silent admission that the fight's been lost.

And like a production line, as one body moves off there, another prepares to move on. It's a frightening thing to watch, especially for those clustered round that bed all day and all night, waiting their turn, hearing the weak groans above them. Seeing the hollowness of those eye sockets sucking in the eyeballs of the dying like quicksand. Watching their mouths fall open, while the flies settle on their blistered lips. They listen hard for that last wisp of breath weakly drawn in, then the final exhale, as that bony chest slowly squeezes out every last bit of air, never to rise again. And the groaning stops. And it's time to call the guards.

I can't let Anna die this way. ARVs have to be bought and I know she doesn't have the money. So I contact one of the missionaries and tell her Anna's story and persuade her to pay for the medication. All Anna has to do is show up at the building once a day, wait for her name to be called and take her tablets.

But when she finds out what I've done, she's fuming. She doesn't want to see me or speak to me. How could I have gone behind her back? Do I want everyone to know she has full-blown AIDS? That's her first admission to me that she's sick. And although I try to convince her that this will save her life, she's too stubborn to listen.

She's also trying to shrug off the stigma attached to AIDS, the idea that it's a punishment for bad behaviour. And I can't be angry with her, although I believe what she's doing is foolish. But we manage to get past our argument and move on. I'm just shocked every time I look at her, that the physical change in her has been so dramatic. She's more dependent on me because her strength is fading. She's struggling to come to terms with this frail, reedy body that can hardly hold food or move around anymore. She goes nowhere without me. And I know that without taking the ARVs, Anna won't last much longer. I contact the embassy to ask them to visit her as soon as possible.

But there's no word from the embassy at all. I'm so angry! How can they possibly abandon one of their own who's so close to the end of her life? I finally get them to contact her family. And a few weeks later, her aunt arrives from South Africa. She waits in the embassy room, while Anna insists I go into the visit with her. I can't. These are two relatives who haven't seen each other for ten years and I don't want to get in their way. But Anna says, if I don't visit with her, she won't go out to see her aunt at all. In her mind, that woman sitting outside may be related to her, but I'm her family. Because as much as our family members care for us, no one knows better than other inmates how it really feels to be stuck here, day after day. I give in, and go into the visit with her.

Her aunt is a woman of few words. And even those spill quietly from her mouth. We all know what this meeting is for. It's Anna's goodbye to her family. Her aunt is emotional but tries to keep it in check. I can see that she knows. She's taken aback at her niece's frailty. I imagine what's going through her head. I sense that all she wants to do is hold Anna in her arms one last time and tell her that she's loved. That the years of distance, and how her actions pushed her family away, don't matter anymore. But that message seems so impossible to convey across wire mesh. As their bodies are kept apart, so too are their souls. Anna asks me to help her out, as her aunt walks away in disappointment.

From that time onwards, Anna grows smaller and sicker every day. But she never makes it onto that bed – that shrine that'll sap the last of her life. The prison authorities suggest she be moved to Klong Prem's hospital. This will be better for her.

On the morning she leaves for Klong Prem, the officers call me in. I find a wheelchair and I settle her into it. She's shrunken, a human raisin, suddenly so old and tiny in this big wheelchair. I push her slowly towards the gates, hear the whirring of the wheels underneath us. I wonder what she's thinking because she doesn't say a word. She doesn't look around, just straight ahead. Focused, it seems, on this goal of dying.

I don't know what to say to her. We both know she's not coming back. So I lean over and hug her gently, hold her in my arms for a moment because I feel her sudden longing to be loved. This woman who was too tough for it all these years before. But I still can't find the words. And nor can she. They take her away. And I say a silent goodbye. Anna is leaving Lard Yao to die.

I'm told she receives fresh flowers from the embassy in Klong Prem hospital. They should've saved them for her funeral. Anna accepts her flowers and is gone. But a Ghanaian prisoner in the ward next door to her comes back to Lard Yao with disturbing news. This woman says she doesn't know what caused Anna such distress towards the end. But in those final moments before she passed, all she did was scream and scream and scream and nobody came and it suddenly went quiet. Maybe Anna was afraid to die alone, just like the rest of us.

This Ghanaian lady brings Anna's things back. Her clothes. A Bible. Some letters and diaries. Usually, if a family can't afford to pay for the remains of their loved ones to be sent home, the missionaries say their prayers and bury the body here in Bangkok. But surprisingly, an embassy official pays for Anna's body to be returned to her family. It's the kindest thing they do for her, even if it is a bit late. But I myself suffer from Anna's death. I feel her absence hang over me as strong as her presence did in the last few months of her life.

And I have this terrible picture in my head of the same thing being done to Anna that was done to the woman who died in Lard Yao hospital next to me. That plugging of holes and sprinkling of powder to repel the ants. And the cruelty of that moment when the Protector arrives the next day, wooden mallet in hand, to lift up that sheet and smash the bones of the woman lying underneath to see if she's really dead or just pretending, before the doctor signs the death certificate.

And once that's confirmed, she's thrown into the back of a van, to lie under a pile of other bodies. And all I see right now is shattered Anna, her broken bones lying cold in a wooden box in the hold of a plane. Her family will get back these pieces of this child they love. They'll try to put her together again, like a puzzle, before her burial. No one ever returns from Lard Yao in one piece. But at least there's one small comfort. After ten horrific years in this human sewer, Anna is finally going home.

CHAPTER 21

Prison love

There are a few things that've pulled me through the years at Lard Yao. The love of God, the love of my child, the love of my family and friends. But one thing I have completely shut out is the love of a man. In prison, there's no room for it anyway. The husbands and boyfriends of the Thai inmates are about the only ones who come here to talk about love. And when you see those meetings, your heart often goes out more to the men than the women. These men with love brimming in their eyes, fighting to keep it alive when they can't even touch their women they've given their lives to. For us foreigners, the chance of finding love in prison is almost zero. The men who could've loved us are never going to entertain relationships with convicted criminals living behind bars.

But there's a man who walks into Lard Yao one day to prove me wrong. He's a complete stranger. Norwegian. Tall at 1.9 metres. Blonde hair and blue-eyes. A heavy accent and beautiful body. And I find it so strange to be looking him up and down, thinking these thoughts again after so many years. His name is Per and he divides his time between working in IT and travelling the world. While in South Africa, he reads a newspaper article about me and makes a mental note to visit me the next time he's in Bangkok. So here he is, out of the blue. Smiling shyly. Making me self-conscious too, because I think I know what he wants from

133

me and I know how ridiculous it is to even consider it.

We visit in the "normal room" for two days – a long, high-ceilinged hall where we sit two metres apart, separated by wire mesh and glass. Thirty prisoners are allowed in at a time and, because of the distance between us and our visitors, we end up shouting at each other for the entire visit, which makes it more comical than romantic. I'm not sure how we feel it but even across this distance, there's some attraction to each other. And as shy as we both are and as embarrassed as I am about being seen by this man in my prison uniform, I suppose we're on our first date. And he comes back the next day for more.

Per travels widely and sends me pictures and postcards a few times a week. He's a romantic soul who can picture me by his side in every place he visits. He has fantasies of us on a beach together in Mozambique swimming with whale sharks. He writes me passionate letters that he decorates with stickers of Cupid and his bow, that make me feel like a teenager enjoying the blush of first love. And he believes with all his heart that this relationship he's imagined will actually be a reality one day. At some stage he comes to Thailand for a whole month and visits me every day. And I ask him repeatedly, "Per, are you sure you want a girlfriend in prison? You don't even know when I'm coming out…" And he brushes me off and says, "There are lots of women on the outside, Vanessa, but there's only one who can win my heart."

I have nothing to lose so I allow Per to become a part of my life. It makes a big difference in here, knowing that there's someone waiting for me on the outside. There's something to look forward to all week with his letters and photos flooding in. And I suddenly find myself thawing, feeling just a bit more human again. Just that little bit happier, so that life in here becomes more tolerable. I fall in love with Per as he has with me.

In January 2006, I'm allowed an inside visit with him. It means I'll actually be able to touch him for the first time and I'm so looking forward to that, although I'm horribly nervous. He sticks out of the crowd, towering above all the visitors, his skin so milky, it seems to reflect the light. And when he sees me, he doesn't say a word. He just enfolds me in his arms and kisses me. His tongue is soft and warm on mine. His touch is comforting. But it's just too much for me. I haven't been touched this way in thirteen years. And when he asks me to kiss him again, I can't.

But there's another side of Per that I find hard to understand. He's jealous and possessive sometimes. He wants to read all my letters to see who they're from. He's worried that I'm having a lesbian relationship with another inmate and cheating on him, which is absurd. And he's hot-headed. One day, he's so upset that he can't touch me because of the Perspex separating us, that he starts banging on it, like he's going to smash it. I have to beg him to stop or the officers will think he's trying to break me out of here. Our relationship continues for six years – until Markus comes along.

You wouldn't think a woman in jail would ever be faced with the choice of which man to love. But there's something about my story that's drawn more than one man here to Lard Yao's gates, hoping to save me from my horrific life. They expect me to be falling to pieces, so battered from this experience that I can hardly stand up. But they're shocked that I seem so normal. What they don't realise is I'm not a new inmate in denial. I've been here for 11½ years. I try to keep my pain to myself. I've survived a broken heart and the separation from my daughter and family. I've lived through the deep depression that almost killed me after my failed pardon. And I've come out on the other side not looking as bad as I could be. I've come to believe there's still a life for me out there one day. And on the day I'm told to pack my bags and go, I want to be ready for that world. I have all my certificates lined up – everything from computer courses to Thai massage courses.

But when Markus comes thundering into my life, he's a stark reminder that the real world is as capable of wounding a human being as prison life is. The day he comes to see me, it's written all over his face. It's in every crease, in every strained expression. In his pained smile, as though he can't forget his sadness for one moment. I understand why. I know his story. How he falls in love with his childhood sweetheart, Marion, and marries her and has a beautiful child. How the cancer begins with just a small spot and spreads like spilt ink throughout her and soils her insides even though Markus is fighting to keep her alive.

He'll do anything. Spend his last cent on medicine from Russia to heal her, to restore her to this woman who never ailed and made memories with him and brought his amazing son into the world. But nothing he does works. When Marion's on her deathbed two days before Christmas, his own soul lies dying there with her. And she takes it with her when she goes. And all that's left is this hollow tree trunk of a man with a child he's raising on his own and a sadness so big, it has its own room in his house.

Markus Gyssler is from Munich, a Berkeley MBA graduate and the CEO of a large German software firm with three hundred employees under him. But he's also a broken man who walks into Lard Yao in pieces, hoping to come and save me the way he never could save his wife. He's found my story on the Prisoners Abroad website run by Kay Danes. He's touched by it and he wants to help me. First he writes to me in December 2006. Then he comes to see me. And the man I see walk in is so much older than his 41 years, a human being so burdened by his past that he can hardly stand up straight.

He visits me in the embassy room for five days and we spend hours talking. Markus wants to know all about me. And I give him the highlights package of the last twelve years of my life. But I really don't want to talk about myself. I have the urge to get *him* to open up. Because he seems such a closed person. Such a sensitive person, clammed up by the hurt. And so I spend many hours of those five days trying to prise that shell open. Pressing him to talk just a little more every day. He admits that he's only spoken to his sister a little about his trauma. But otherwise, he carries it himself. And it's slowly destroying him. Aside from his son, it seems he has no other reason to go on living.

I know I need to help him somehow. It feels to me like he came here, not to rescue me, but to be rescued by me. I suddenly feel personally responsible for this man. As though, in these few days I have with him, I have to do something to make him realise that he has to go on after the death of his wife, that he has to find joy in life again or he might as well be dead. It's a lesson I've had to learn too. He resists talking about his problems at first. But when he sees I'm determined to hear every detail of his story, he slowly, cautiously opens up.

Markus relives everything about his love for his wife, for his half-orphaned child. He spares no detail. He chokes. He breaks down and he cries uncontrollably. And how I wish I could reach across the bars and comfort him. But he comes back, again and again for five days and he does the same thing. He talks and cries and cries until eventually he smiles. And on the fifth day, there's a different man who walks in. A man without that pain trapped in his eyes. He leaves lighter, feeling a release – this man who walked in as a stranger less than a week ago and is leaving today as my friend.

I feel a deep connection to Markus. And he feels it too. He says to me one day, "Vanessa, you're a very unselfish person. Despite all the suffering you've been through, you're still able to put my problems before yours." And all I can say is how grateful I am that he chose to share them with me. We begin a relationship that's forged in something so much deeper than just flirtation. He believes I've saved his life because this visit has changed him radically. And I believe that Markus is somehow beginning to save mine with the depth of his feeling and how involved he becomes in my life.

In the months that follow, he deposits money into my account and sends me so many necessities I used to have to do without. He visits me every three months. Although he's seven years older than me, our birthdays are just one day apart, on the 17th and 18th of December, so he makes sure he's there every year to somehow make my birthday special. He arrives with a birthday hat for me, and various trimmings. One year he even puts on the head of a chicken costume and dances around idiotically in the embassy room until I'm almost crying with laughter! There is this light-hearted side of him that can turn serious in an instant. And in the months that follow, it's this side I see. He asks me if it's alright if he gets to know my family and friends. He contacts Melanie, Felicia and my mother, and he offers them any help they may need.

There is something stable about Markus. He becomes an anchor in my life, a go-between who keeps me in greater contact with my life in South Africa and my daughter. He's an efficient, focused, persistent man and this is part of what attracts me to him. In time, Felicia gets to know him well. He visits Melanie and my family and introduces himself as my close friend, which he truly is by now. And I suddenly know that I love Markus deeply. He commits himself to me as I am in this prison. But he also commits himself to the woman I am outside of here. The mother, the daughter, the friend. He flies to Bangkok with Felicia three times. And each time, she speaks of his kindness to her. Of how she can share things with him about her life that she sometimes finds it difficult to talk to anyone else about. One weekend in Bangkok, Felicia gets ill. Her tonsils worry her and she's up all night. Markus doesn't get a wink of sleep either because he spends hours awake, nursing her.

It's a long time before I find the courage to tell Per about Markus. I feel so guilty about the way this has turned out and I don't want to hurt Per's feelings. But the day they both visit me in jail, Per in the morning, Markus in the afternoon, I know I can't let this continue. So I tell Per the truth and I break his heart. Like every man who's lost his girlfriend to someone else, he wants to know what Markus has that he hasn't. But it's not something I can easily explain. What Markus and I have shared has touched both of us to the core of our souls. And I know I'll never have that with Per. But he's not a bitter person. He still holds out some hope and visits me from time to time. We remain friends over the years.

Markus, though, is now longing for a much deeper commitment – one I could never have dreamt of in this jail. He wants to marry me, right here, behind bars and he even gets official permission to go ahead. This is not the way I'd hoped it would happen. I'd imagined a wedding somewhere romantic, where we say our vows in front of a priest, not a prison director, and Markus puts a ring on my finger as a free woman. But when he brings me that ring that sparkles so delicately in the prison light and goes on his knees with such sincerity, I just say yes without thinking about it a second longer. He's overjoyed. But I'm shocked more than anything. After everything I've lost in here – my freedom, my dignity, my child, the last thing I ever thought I'd find was love in Lard Yao.

CHAPTER 22

Amnesty

"Five – you sure it's five?"

"Yes, yes. Five."

I'm running between buildings, breathless, tripping over my own feet, my sledgehammer heart pounding so loudly inside my chest, I'm sure all these officers blurring past me must be able to hear it. I grab another warder walking past.

"Did I hear correctly? Five, is that right?"

She's doing a mental calculation, her eyes rolling about in her sockets. *Hurry up!*

"Yes, you right. Five."

But it's not enough. I tear around the corner, panting, gasping for breath, almost crashing into another officer. I'm so choked up, I can hardly get the words out.

"Subtract... for me... please..." I say.

"Yes, five right," she nods, certain of it. "You happy?"

Happy? My head is thrown back. I'm laughing! My outstretched arms are touching heaven, and I'm showering my joy on Lard Yao in this moment, drowning out its misery in this crazy, head-spinning moment that's crashed upon me, sent my mind swimming, my heart gushing, my body hurtling through these corridors to make sure it's actually true! My friends fling themselves at me like lit grenades, exploding in my arms, ecstatic, hysterical, grateful, delighted, jumping, screaming, crying. And I'm shouting, "I can't believe it! I just can't believe it! Oh God! Thank you, God! Thank you for hearing me!" And the tears are streaming from my face and there's a lump in my throat the size of a boulder, because today, 14 December 2009, a miracle's happened. A miracle I've prayed and begged and cried for and never stopped hoping for, every minute I've spent in this place.

I am leaving Lard Yao in five months! In less than half a year, I'll be a free woman again! I can almost taste the freedom on my tongue. It's cool and sweet and thirst quenching. And I'm as impatient as the deserts for rain, wishing this day would come tomorrow! Wishing I could close my eyes and force myself five months to the day when I leave Lard Yao – not in a wheelchair or a body bag, but strong, on my own two feet, step by step, turning my back on the most horrific time of my life. It's been a long, painful race that's lasted fifteen years. Fifteen years that have felt more like thirty. A race that's bent my body, my mind, my soul beyond their limits. I came into this place a naïve 22 year-old. But when I leave, I'll be someone else – not that young woman driven here in an overcrowded bus so many years ago, who knew almost nothing about life. This jail has done its worst to me, but I'm still standing. And when I walk out, I'll be Thirty-seven-year-old Vanessa, free woman, survivor of the worst women's prison in Thailand.

Today is nine days after the King's birthday. It's the only birthday we consider more important than our own because he often celebrates it with amnesties for prisoners. The morning of the announcement, we chat eagerly among ourselves and try to guess who may have won the King's favour. And as we're debating this, the prison officials call us together to make the official announcement. And I'm standing there nervously, my hands shaking, my eyes clenched because I'm so desperate to hear whether my sentence has been reduced.

And then I hear it above the other women's cheers. "Drugs cases: a two-year reduction in sentence." And that feels like my magic lottery-winning number! I just know without even doing the sums, what it means. And while the tears flood my eyes, I smile through them. I feel myself lifted, buoyed above all these people, above all these buildings, as though I can already see over them into the world outside. And I see the *gong li un* and remember the promise made there on the 18th of March 1995, when I sat, surrounded by Christian worshippers. It was almost a year since I'd come to Lard Yao. Exhausted, despairing, spent. A young prisoner-mother without hope. And I can still see myself weeping, asking Lisa Taylor, the preacher, "If I accept God, will he open the door for me to go home?" And she says, "Yes, he'll open the door for you, but I can't say when. I only know he can strengthen you to deal with this situation for as long as you're here." And I know that's the promise I've survived on, for more than fifteen years in this place.

Today there's such excitement in this prison. Some of us have had our sentences shortened. Others have won their freedom. We are children, celebrating this simple act of going home, that everyone outside these walls takes for granted every day. Over the years, the King's amnesties have brought me some hope. An amnesty is important because even if you've been refused a pardon, there's still hope that an amnesty can lower your prison sentence by decades. You don't have to apply for it and there are no costs involved. You're purely at the mercy of the King.

This is how I go from serving a life sentence to a term of just over 18 years. It's a long, confusing process that begins with the death sentence I receive in 1994. It's immediately commuted to life in prison because I have a baby, but then I make two appeals. The first one fails and my life sentence is confirmed. But when it goes on appeal again in 1996, two years after I've landed in Lard Yao, my sentence is drastically reduced to thirty-five years.

Just two days after this court appearance, it's the King's birthday and he offers me my first amnesty which reduces my jail term by another five years, leaving me with thirty years to serve in Lard Yao. But following that, there are four more amnesties from the King, and each time I find my sentence whittled down by a few years until I have eighteen years, six months and sixteen days of my jail term left. I've already served more than fifteen years of that, so it means all I have left in Lard Yao is just over two years.

And that's why I've been dashing through these corridors like a crazed woman today, begging every officer I can find to help me work out the meaning of this. Checking that my calculations are correct because I don't want to accept this as the truth until I know for sure it is. The disappointment would be too great. I even contact the embassy to confirm that I'll be going home in five months. And they say yes, that's correct. You'll be home in five months. And I scream some more and I cry. And I keep saying to myself, "Vanessa, you're going home, you're finally going home!"

There are thousands of us whose sentences have been reduced, so it takes the officials at Lard Yao three months to update the prison cards that we clip onto our uniforms every day. The new card reflects my new sentence. The best thing about being released at this time is that I will walk out of Lard Yao a day before Felicia's sixteenth birthday – 30 October 2010. The last one I celebrated with her was her third, which she probably doesn't even remember anymore. Thirteen lost birthdays with my daughter. I have so much to make up for. I recall her third birthday party in this prison, how I watched her blow out her candles and felt the light going out in me because I knew I was moments away from losing her. And I imagine myself at her next party. What a joy and privilege it'll be to actually be there instead of reading about it in a letter from home or staring at pictures for hours imagining that I was there too.

In the meantime, I swing wildly between emotions. I cry when it hits me that I'll soon be home. And sometimes I laugh for the same reason. I count the days, I cross them off the calendar. I beg them to march on steadily towards the New Year, to jump forward to the end of October. But this excitement and eagerness to turn my back on Lard Yao starts to sew a mild panic in me. And that soon grows like a wave that rolls towards me so hard, I'm afraid it'll wash me away. I suddenly start to torture myself with a whole lot of questions: Am I actually capable of doing this? Living in the real world again? This is all I've known for more than a decade. These high walls and this compound inside them have been my whole world for so long. I feel like I know nothing beyond here. That taking one step onto that street outside would be stepping onto the surface of another planet where there's no oxygen.

And as much hatred as I've had for Lard Yao every moment I've walked on its soil, this is my home. I've tried to deny it forever. But I can't any longer. Lard Yao *is* my home. It has been for more than a decade and a half. These Thais I despised for what they'd done to me – they're now my family. And all of a sudden, after my desperation to go back to my country and the people I've loved and longed for all these years, I'm afraid they'll feel like complete strangers to me. I haven't seen my mother, Melissa or Jacky for over fifteen years. When I left, Melanie was my friend, not the mother of my child. And Collette and Christine? What will I say to them? How should I behave around them? Will they look at me and think how much I've changed? How old I look, how strangely I talk? I haven't slept on a bed for so long, or felt hot water running over my body for years. Can I go back home and pretend I'm not some kind of savage who's forgotten how to live as a normal human being?

I'm scared. So scared of what will be expected of me. How will I learn to be a mother to Felicia after all these years? She calls me Vanessa and Melanie "Mom" because during a prison visit some years ago, I told her to. I had to. I truly felt Melanie had become her real mother. When Felicia was sick or sad, or struggling with life, I wasn't there to parent her. Melanie's earned the right to be called "Mom". It's a title she deserves after all she's given up for Felicia and me. But if she's Mom, I don't know who I'll be to Felicia or where I'll fit in or what I'll be expected to do and say. And the thought that Felix will be part of the package and I'll be forced to see him again drives me mad because I'm still so angry with him after all these years.

I don't even know my home anymore. People tell me amazing things about South Africa. How it's changed so radically since I've been away. How politics and the new laws and the high crime rate are part of South African life. And somewhere inside I'm excited about seeing the change for myself. But I'm also afraid I'll go back and look at all the old places and everything I remember will be wiped out and replaced with something new and I'll feel like a foreigner in the country of my birth. And how will I find work there – especially if people believe I've committed a crime? I'm told there are so many South Africans – highly qualified people who've been to university – without jobs. With my background, who will want to employ me?

Work and Felicia and family and friends and South Africa and Markus and me. It's all too much! I can't stand these thoughts rushing at me, mobbing me, pinning me to the ground, kicking me in the head. All of a sudden I'm terrified of leaving here! I don't want to stay here anymore but I'm too scared to go. Is it really possible that my home could be more frightening than Lard Yao? Am I off my head that I'd want to stay here instead of going home? What the hell is wrong with me? I can't sleep anymore because these thoughts are buzzing so loudly around me at night, stinging me hard. And I'm constantly nervous. I can't eat. The panic attacks start again. I'm losing control. I can feel all the progress I've made slipping from my grasp. I have to do it. I have to start taking the pills again even though I don't want to. Markus buys them for me. I shove them down my throat every day, swallow hard, just so this madness will end. And slowly, calmly, over several weeks, I manage to bring some of my thoughts and fears under control.

Markus is worried about me, but he's also ecstatic that I'll be a free woman in just a few months' time. We've held off getting married until I can get out of here and he's looking forward to us sharing a life together outside of the shackles of prison love. He talks me through my periods of anxiousness. He comforts me and reminds me that he'll never leave my side once I'm out there. And that's what I need to hear. That Markus will be my armour in the real world. But he does more than just reassure me that everything will be fine. A few months before my release, he goes to my family and friends in South Africa and prepares them for my homecoming. And suddenly, the bush is beaten back, the sunlight streams in and a path is carved out for me by my kind, caring Markus who always manages to think of everything.

With some of the pressure off me, I decide I'll allow myself a little bit of vanity. I have no clothes to wear when I leave prison. Much of what I came here with has been stolen. I have to lay my hands on something new, so I look the part of a free woman when I walk out of here. I can't wait to become invisible in that crowd once I step out onto the streets. There will be no more uniform to mark me. Nothing that says to anyone I'm a convicted criminal. An officer thoughtfully buys me a pair of shoes, which wrap around my feet snugly and will proudly carry me out of here. I feel like I should splash out on myself so I show another officer a picture in a magazine of an outfit Victoria Beckham is wearing. It's a smart-casual pants suit. I tell her I love it and I want to walk to my freedom in it! She has it made outside the prison for me. I lock it away carefully for my big day.

For now, I try not to think of the big things. I focus on the small things that I know with certainty will make me happy out there in that alien world. Touching my hand to my child's beautiful face. Smothering my mother in a hug. Tasting Aunty Rushda's food. Walking on an empty beach with Markus. But I have another wish that's so simple, I'm almost too shy to tell anyone. Every night I've been locked in these cells for 15 years, I've yearned for just one glimpse of the night sky with its scatter of stars. And I decide that when I'm free, that's all I'll do at night. Lie under those magical stars studded high above me and wish and wish my life back to normal.

CHAPTER 23

Departures

Melanie is dead.

Melanie with her echoing laughter, her shrill voice and crazy sense of humour; Melanie who used to break into her stepdad's liquor cabinet when we were teenagers and get us all tipsy; Melanie who believed in my innocence and opened her big heart and took my little Felicia in when she was forced out of her prison nest. That Melanie – the sister-friend I love with all my heart, is gone. Why? Why couldn't she wait? At 37, she can't have been ready for death. I know she was waiting with such impatience for me to come home, so excited, so looking forward to sharing this precious child who's now both of ours. Her spirit may have longed for it. But her body gave in. And there's no way of undoing any of it.

It's June. Father's Day – just over three months to my release. But today Melanie's not her usual self. She's irritable and short-tempered. She fights with everyone in the house over something or other. Felicia complains of a sore foot and Melanie tells her to walk to the chemist. "But I have a sore foot. How can I walk there?" she asks. Melanie's unreasonable, so Lerell, her daughter, feels sorry for Felicia and they walk there together and buy some ointment that they're not sure will help anyway. And in typical teenager style, when Felicia comes back, she decides she'll be angry with Melanie for two weeks for what she's done. She's not sure why it has to be exactly that long, but it feels just right to her. Then Melanie walks in and says sorry, sadly, sincerely and suddenly she's Felicia's whole world again and they make up and go to church together in the evening with the rest of the family.

But when she comes back, Melanie complains of chest pains and takes a tablet for some relief. But it only gets worse, until she can't stand it anymore and starts screaming with pain. At this moment, everyone's paralysed – the whole family. They're standing and staring and no one knows what to do for her – except Felicia. My daughter springs into action and says, "We have to do something to help her!" And this suddenly gets the room moving, everyone running. They'll take her to her sister, Dolly, who's a nurse.

Melanie's bundled into the car and driven to Dolly's house. And on the way, she grabs Felicia's hand. Doesn't just hold it – she clasps it in a death grip. Felicia tries to smooth out Melanie's fingers, to relax them, because they suddenly feel so steely, so cold and stiff. But the moment she straightens them, they spring back into that curved grip, which frightens Felicia so much. And as they're getting there, she leans towards Felicia and says, "Pray for me". And my child promises she will. And those are the last words Melanie ever says to Felicia, because she's hauled into Dolly's house and off to the hospital from there.

Melanie's treated so badly when she gets to hospital. She's admitted, but the nurses don't bother attending to her right away. She's gasping for breath because the pain is crushing her chest, squeezing all the air out of her lungs. But when the nurses eventually come back, they wheel her into another room and leave her there, alone. There's no doctor on duty. She'll have to wait for one. And by the time that happens, by the time she makes it into Intensive Care, Melanie's already past the point of saving.

Felicia only gets to the hospital once Melanie's rigged up to all the tubes and pipes and machines. She looks at her lying in that bed and struggles to see her mother there. She's more robotic than human, taken over by these twisting, beeping pieces of plastic and metal all creeping out of her, like vines into plugs at the wall. And somehow that gives Felicia distance from this scene in front of her.

Makes her believe for a moment that this isn't really Melanie lying there. Just someone who looks like her, who can't seem to breathe on her own. And the family begins singing for comfort. That's what they do when things get hard. They sing their Christian songs and hope their voices are heard. But Felicia can't stand it. She wants to shut out the strains of their music. These sound like funeral songs, inviting death into this place. "Stop it!" she says and walks away.

She's standing out there for a few moments, gathering her thoughts, when a team of nurses and doctors rushes past her with some noisy equipment. Its wheels make a racket on the floor. She suddenly realises they're heading for Melanie. But before they get to her bed, Felicia feels something. A quiet slipping away through the crack of a door left slightly ajar. Her hand slowly being let go off. Gently, just a whiff of vanishing. And Felicia knows Melanie's flown this place. She doesn't cry. A peace comes over her. She's okay with it. She's relieved that Melanie went without too much of a struggle. On the whole, it all happened pretty fast. And that's probably how Melanie would've planned it herself.

There's wailing behind Felicia. And she can't stand the sound of that either. It's somehow more upsetting to her than Melanie's death. She knows Melanie never liked a display. Remembers going home with her after a funeral and Melanie saying in her usual cheeky way, "Do me a favour. When I die, please don't cry for me like that – it's embarrassing!" And suddenly everyone's laughing although they've just spent the last few hours bawling at the side of someone's grave. Felicia won't wail the way the others do. She'll respect Melanie's wishes.

The tubes have all been removed and Felicia's called back in to say goodbye to Melanie. Lerell is draped over her mother's body, crying loudly. There's sorrow everywhere. It's hanging in this ward like thick smoke. It chokes Felicia. She wants to say goodbye. But not like this. She'd rather stand back. Let the others have their moment with Melanie before she says a quiet goodbye. Death doesn't drill to the core of her like it does to the others. Maybe it's because she spent her first three years in a place where death was such a frequent visitor. But when she's called and asked to say goodbye to Melanie, Felicia walks up to the edge of the bed and touches her feet. They're still warm. As though she's still alive. And touching her feet – that's Felicia's last act of respect for a woman who's given her everything for more than thirteen years. It's how Felicia says goodbye.

At the funeral, Felicia somehow zones out. She watches it all unfold like a movie. There's a coffin and singing and prayers and more tears. But she promised Melanie years ago that if anything happened to her, she'd take over. She'd make sure that all the others were okay – Hilton, Lerell, their little sister Tatum. Felicia's used to separation, to disappointment. She's come to understand that people are only in her life for seasons anyway. That relationships, even with people you love, are never permanent. Life is too changeable for that. Felicia somehow manages to blot out everything. Almost falls asleep on her feet at the funeral and then suddenly wakes up at the graveyard, and there's a big hole and people are throwing sand into it and it hits her for the first time that it really is Melanie lying at the bottom of that hole – the woman she called "Mom" ever since she can remember. Melanie is dead. It finally sinks in. And she's completely devastated.

A few days after Melanie's death, Mrs Holmes, the woman who's visited prisoners in Thailand for 20 years, comes to the prison for a weekly visit with me. And just the way she walks in tells me there's something terribly wrong. "Hi, Vanessa, can you sit down?" she asks. "Let's pray first." And before I've had a chance to interrupt, she's already begun "Lord, please give Vanessa strength and help her…" I hear nothing else. My eyes are open. The worst thoughts are flashing through my head. What's happened? Is it Felicia, is it Markus? I can't take any more bad news. Not now. Not so close to going home.

Mrs Holmes opens her eyes. "Markus called me last night," she says. "He was crying a lot. He really wanted to be here for you and comfort you today. This will come as a shock to you. I'm so sorry to have to tell you this. Melanie's passed away."

"No!" I'm shaking my head. That can't be. No, not Melanie. That's impossible.

"Are you sure? Are you sure about the name?" I keep on asking her. "Melanie is so young, she's fit and healthy... It just can't be, Mrs Holmes..."

But she's nodding her head. So sure of herself. "Yes, it is Melanie. There's no mistake. She complained about a pain in her chest. She was rushed to the hospital, but she died of a heart attack a few hours later," she says.

I have nothing more to say. All I know is I don't want to believe those words. I choose not to believe them as though this will change the fact of Melanie's death. I'm shocked. I'm rooted there. The words are stuck in my throat, any clear thoughts wiped from my mind. It makes no sense to me, this news. I can't accept it as fact yet. Someone, somewhere along the chain, got the message wrong. Inserted Melanie's name instead of someone else's. I'm so convinced of this that I go back to the computer room and continue with my work. I mention to my colleagues there that I've heard Melanie's dead. They come over to comfort me but I don't really need it. I keep telling them I'm fine because I am. She can't be dead.

But that state of numbness can't last forever. That night, I'm restless. I dream that someone's lying behind me. And I know it's Melanie. She's naked. I reach back to put my hand on her shoulder. But when I touch her, she's ice cold. I burst out of that dream, terrified. I jump up and the tears are streaming down my face. I cry all night long into the next day. Melanie *is* dead. And all I ask is, "God, how could you allow this to happen?"

There's so much I never got to say to Melanie. A backlog of sixteen and a half years of gratitude, of love that I so wanted to share with Melanie for all she did for Felicia and me. And she dies now, on the verge of my homecoming. Just three and a half months more, Melanie. Couldn't you wait? You'd already waited nearly sixteen and a half years. What's three more months? It always bothered me when she came here that she never really knew how I felt. It was like all my words of thanks got caught in that wire mesh and stayed there. I never got to hug and thank her so she could physically feel how grateful I was. I won't even be there to

151

say it at her funeral, so I do the best I can. I come together with all the prisoners and warders whose hearts she touched during every visit and we hold our own memorial service for Melanie.

We have beautiful, funny stories to tell about how she'd always arrive with bucketfuls of KFC for me to share with the other prisoners and treats for the warders who were good to me. When Melanie came, everyone had something to look forward to. And at the memorial service, we cry when we think of her generosity and softness of heart. We cry for her wider family that will struggle to hold itself together now that their glue is gone. And I weep quietly for Felicia who's lost her second mother in such a short life-span. My heart breaks for Hilton, Lerell and Tatum who couldn't have been blessed with a better mother. But at this service, we also laugh. We laugh when we recall Melanie's honesty – how she comforts you in one sentence and tells you what a drama queen you are in the next! How she lines up with the girls and does a special farewell "Macarena" dance for me before they go, leaving the officers in stitches. I miss Melanie terribly, achingly. She's sewn light wherever she walked. And that's why, in my mind, she'll never be dead, only absent. And I try to keep her voice alive in my memory by re-reading all the letters she sent me.

"Dear Nessa, I know how much you long for freedom and miss your child terribly. It's not fair that you two can't be together. I sat down when we came back to South Africa and cried. I was so deeply hurt, I felt so much pain, like a knife cutting straight through my heart. I pray for you every day and I know God is going to bring you through this and bring everyone together. I know it feels like it's taking forever, the longing, the pain, the tears, but in the end it is all going to be worth it..."

I cling to that hope. But all I want to do now is take my child in my arms. It kills me that I can't be there to comfort her. Tell her that this is not the way it's meant to be. That in some people's lives it is different. The people they love don't just come and go. Their mothers don't have to kick them out when they're three years old. Their fathers always stay a part of their lives. But what will any of that mean to her? She's never known life to be that generous or stable. Every conversation I've had with her when she's come here with Markus tells me that my child lives on change. Thrives on it. Expects the details of her life to change the way the weeks do after every seven days. It's too late to teach her otherwise.

It's a lesson I'm learning too. But I'm still grieving for Melanie, when more bad news comes in a month before I leave Lard Yao. This time, it's about my sister, Jacky. There's been an accident. Jacky's standing on the stairs at home when her pet dog jumps on her. She tips over and loses her balance. Goes flying down the stairs. She breaks her ankle, but the pain is so severe, she has to be taken to hospital. All Jacky knows is pain anyway. You'd think she'd be used to it by now, know it intimately, like a friend who never leaves her side. But her body's had enough. She has a heart attack. And on 29 September, Jacky dies when she's just 40 years old. My sister and I have become strangers over the years. I console myself by thinking that she truly deserved some relief, some peace from all her problems, and I hope she's finally managed to find it.

Now, I sit in Lard Yao, on the threshold of my release. I'm going home to find more pain. What was I expecting? That this framed portrait of my old life hanging in my head was going to look the same more than sixteen years on? Now, there are two gaping holes where Melanie and Jacky stood. I feel a sudden desperation to get home right now. I must stop this merciless cutting away of the branches of my life that grow beyond the shadows of Lard Yao.

CHAPTER 24

Leaving Lard Yao

I open my eyes. It's 30 October 2010. The light is somehow different today. Fresh, new and soft as though there's never been a day like it before. And there's something bubbling in the pit of me. A cocktail of nervousness, uncertainty, joy, anticipation. Today, I am to become a free woman.

The days leading up to this day have been hard. I so desperately want to go, but the thought that I'm leaving behind so many wonderful, broken women who need me is hard to accept. I speak to each one of them and say goodbye. But the words don't come easily. What can I say to women who are sitting here without the hope I now have? Many of them have no idea when they're going home. So all I can do is share with them how I feel. "I've watched people go like this. And I've waited for my day," I tell them. "Today is my day in the same way that your day is going to come. And this is my prayer: I'm opening the gate for the foreigners. And that's the prayer I pray to God – that as I walk out of here, you will follow."

I'm torn between leaving my friends behind and returning to the love of my family who've been waiting for so many years to have me back home. They've staked so much on this hope. But I am filled with so many mixed feelings. I don't know how to feel. I cry, I laugh, I doubt myself, I'm scared. I have moments of confidence. I try not to be over-eager because it's possible that this is all a mistake. A few years ago, they announced an amnesty when there was none. And I've also seen the wrong woman released and re-arrested a few days later so the right prisoner can go free. That's why I won't allow myself to believe I'm free until I'm on a plane to South Africa.

My name is called and I'm told I must be at the administrative offices by 9am; I am filled with hope. The cell door opens to spit me out for the last time. I shower in ice cold water for the last time. I get dressed for the first time in so many years, not in my prison uniform, but in the clothes of a free woman – this black and white suit that I've been waiting to put on for weeks now. And at 9am promptly, I'm at the administrative building having my fingerprints taken one last time. I'm given a wad of release papers in Thai to sign. I happily do so without reading them. Today, all I care about is my freedom.

Suddenly, in their eyes, I am human. The officers treat me with respect. They offer me a chair to sit on and a plate of food, some rice with soya mince, to eat with a fork. But I can't swallow one mouthful. I'm too wound up to eat anything. They open the safe and bring out my jewellery – the ring, the chain I was wearing all those years ago when I was arrested – Felix's gifts. They still have a few of the one- and two-rand coins that were in my purse. I try on the ring and it still fits. I put the chain around my neck. But it feels so strange, this cold metal on my skin. I can hardly believe that I'm actually wearing jewellery again after all these years. But I don't keep it on for long. The ring is heavy on my finger. The chain weighs like a noose around my neck.

I step outside and the street is so busy. There are cars and tuk tuks zooming by, people so caught up in their conversations they don't even see me standing there. There's a tree outside and some noisy birds settling on its branches. Ordinary, normal life. It floods me with such happiness. Plants such a broad smile on my face. The officers bring me something to drink while I'm standing outside, waiting for my transport to the Immigration Detention Centre. I should be going to the police station first, but my close friend, Collette, a magistrate in South Africa, has fought the system hard and persuaded the authorities that I must go straight to Immigration because there's a high risk of being raped at the police station, where I'll have to present myself alone. No one is allowed to go through this process with me. Thai law prescribes that a prisoner has to scale this last hurdle alone.

And when the car pulls up in front of me, I focus only on getting my bags in and settling myself into the seat. I don't look sideways and I especially don't look back. I don't need one last glance at my humiliating past. The officer who fetches me is chatty. He knows of foreigners who leave this prison and never get to Immigration because they don't want to leave. They're dropped off somewhere in the middle of Bangkok and disappear for good. I can sense he's offering me this option. But besides being illegal, why would I want to stay here? I can almost hear my country calling.

I feel dizzy and nauseous travelling by car; the smell of petrol makes me want to hurl. It's been so long since I last went anywhere in a car. We pull up outside the Immigration Detention Centre. It's painted a stark white with yellow trimmings that look like they were added afterwards to give it a more cheerful feel. I already have a plane ticket that Markus bought me so I'm hoping this process won't take too long. But it's already Friday afternoon. The officials are trickling home. And the one woman who should be on duty to help me has already left for the weekend. She'll be back on Monday.

I'm so discouraged. I'd really hoped I could get out of here this weekend. But the officers on duty say they'll have to check on my plane ticket, find out exactly which plane I'll be travelling on and do a full security check before I leave. They lead me to a room that looks like a hospital ward. It's called Room 1. There are two young South Korean women in there who look upset that I'll be sharing their space. I stay there until the evening. Then the officers take a picture of me and lead me upstairs to Room 11.

It's not really a room, but more a large, overcrowded jail cell, bursting with foreigners of all kinds. Children, women, men. All stuffed into this filthy area with the usual half-exposed toilets at the side. Blankets line the floors. Washing hangs along sagging lines against the walls. There's the smell of human waste in the air. Sweat and urine bubbling through pores. I want to know who these people are. The officer says many are foreigners who've been here for years. A lot of them are refugees. They have no money, no visa or passport to go home. So they live out their days in these conditions. Some of them will die here. Others will eventually find their way home if someone takes pity on them and buys them a plane ticket. All I know is, I can't stay here. I won't. This is the life I've just walked away from. I've more than paid my dues. I won't let anyone treat me this way ever again.

"No," I say to him firmly. "I refuse to stay in there. Take me downstairs. I have a headache and I don't feel well." He's surprised at how abrupt I am but he doesn't have the energy to argue. He takes me back to the room with the two girls in it. They tell him in Thai, not knowing I understand every word falling from their mouths, that I don't belong here and he should take me back upstairs. So he tries to get me to go back to Room 11. But I threaten to call my embassy and he gives in.

I stand my ground. Although two other foreigners arrive and are taken straight up to Room 11, I stay in the hospital room on Friday and Saturday. When my embassy representative gets there on Sunday, I tell her that I've refused to stay in Room 11. She's already had Collette barking at her over the phone from South Africa and doesn't want to risk another scolding. She tells the Immigration Officer to leave me in here and start processing my papers. She promises me it'll take three days to get through this. In reality, it takes five days.

But in this time, at least I manage to see some of the people who've been a great source of strength to me throughout my time in prison. Several friends and missionaries, like Mrs Holmes, visit me. They bring me food, which I gladly share with the others being kept in the room. They also give me clothes, shoes and other necessities for my trip home.

On Sunday, I get a huge surprise when the embassy official and Markus arrive together. It's Felicia's birthday and I'm desperate to speak to her. But I don't know how to use a cellphone, so the embassy lady makes the call and hands the phone to me. "Happy birthday!" I shout as soon as Felicia answers. And all she can say is, "Oh my God. Oh my God!" And she starts to cry and she hands the phone over to Hilton who cries too and sets me off. Markus holds something glinting in his hand and he quickly slips it onto my finger. If we weren't properly engaged before, we are now.

On my last day there, the officers let me out for two hours to walk around the yard. There's a little shop there, where phone cards are sold. I buy one and a Malaysian woman at the centre shows me how to use it.

I'm so excited! I haven't spoken on a phone in over sixteen years! I don't know what I'm going to say yet, but I dial my mother's number first. I try several times, but I can't get through. Then I try Aunty Rushda's number but the call won't go through either. I'm so bitterly disappointed. I decide to try Aunty Rushda's sister, Verna, in Cape Town in case she's available. And sure enough, after a few rings, she picks up and I'm thrilled to hear her familiar voice on the other side. But she can't believe it's me. She bombards me with a whole lot of questions: "Where are you? Where are you calling from? Are you in the prison?"

And I'm shouting back, "No, I'm free! I'm coming home!"

"You're coming home?" And the line suddenly goes dead. I call back and she tells me she thought my first call was a prank call and that's why she hung up. She's so excited about my news. I ask her to please call my mom and Aunty Rushda and tell them I'm coming home. And just saying those simple words makes me so emotional.

I pack up my things and when I'm ready to leave, they ask me if I have petrol money for the officer to take me to the airport. I'll hand over every last cent I have to get there if needs be. On the way there, the officer stops to fetch two more men. I'm uncomfortable in this car surrounded by these strange men. But I feel better when he drops the two of them off before we reach the airport. And when we get there and he parks the car, I look up at the signage and the doors and I'm reminded of how I left here sixteen and a half years ago. Handcuffed. The angel officer's jersey wrapped around my wrists to hide my shame. The prying eyes that drilled into me because they knew better than me how justice works in Thailand.

Today, the officers are kind to me at the airport. There's a whole delegation of about twenty people waiting for me here, and although I'm not really allowed visitors, the officers let them in and allow us some time together to say goodbye. It's more or less the same group that visited me in the Immigration Detention Centre a few days ago. But now, there's a real finality to this meeting. We all know that with a criminal record, I can never return to Thailand again. And I don't know how to thank these men and women who came into my life at different times to save me, to uplift me, to carry me sometimes when I couldn't drag myself to my feet. We take pictures. We pray together. We clasp each other and cry. They're so happy for me. They've worked and prayed so hard for my freedom, and today we know someone's been listening.

Markus arrives. And I'm so happy to see him. I run towards him. I touch him. And he instantly goes from being my phantom boyfriend behind the glass to this living, breathing, solid human being. We hold each other. I cling to him. I can't believe this is really happening! Markus does the practical stuff. He packs my bags and gets my papers in order while I stand there thinking, remembering things from the past. I see the police manning their scanners, going through the luggage of every passenger with such care. And there's my younger self, so many years earlier, desperate to leave Bangkok for home. I see my bag and the scanner and the books. I see the Man in Green and Black and his sharp pocket knife. I see the fine dust of heroin in the air. And I hear him say "Just one minute" like they all do as a habit in Thailand. We head for the Interrogation Room together. And how that one fleeting moment turns into sixteen and a half years of anguish. Years that changed my life, changed me forever.

But I can't keep standing here, locked into my thoughts. Markus takes my hand and guides me to Immigration. He has to leave me there. I sit and wait patiently while the wheels of bureaucracy turn slowly. Then an officer tells me it's time to go. He walks me across the steaming tarmac to the plane and Markus is waiting for me there. I only have an emergency passport and they're full of questions. But thankfully, Markus has the strength to explain it all because I certainly don't. I know I'd never have made it this far without him.

And as I walk up those stairs, all I can think about is how strange this is to me. Unreal. The places I've been, the new people I've met in the last few days. It's more than I've had to take in, for years. And when the engines are fired and the air hostess stands in front, waving her arms in funny directions, I don't listen to a word she says. My mind is floating backwards to all those nights I lay in my jail cell, listening to these huge engines roaring in the sky, hungering to be here. Desperate to sit among the passengers treating this as just another overseas trip, notching up their traveller miles.

Markus leans over and makes sure I'm strapped in tight. The earth seems to shudder beneath me and we're taxiing along, the runway lights flashing every few metres on either side of the plane. We gain speed and the tyres hug the tarmac and suddenly I feel it – that lurch in the pit of my stomach as we lift off the ground and we're soaring, head-first towards the sky. And this moment is so huge for me, so thrilling, I can't hold back anymore. While the engines scream and we climb higher, higher, the tears flood my eyes, pour down my face. "Oh God! This is finished!" I cry. "They can't take me back now. I'm on my way home. I'm really going home!" And I turn to him to dry my tears – this man who's been so strong for me all along the way. But Markus, he's crying too.

CHAPTER 25

Coming home

My home is not my home anymore. I'm a foreigner here. An outsider. Just like everyone else who lands here and admires this place but doesn't have South Africa in their blood, like I thought I did. Sixteen and a half years. That's how long I've yearned for my country. Craved just a small taste of the people, the food, the languages, this sky that stretches over us like God's umbrella.

But now I'm here. Standing at the airport. OR Tambo International, which was called Jan Smuts when I left in 1994, with its high roof and gleaming marble that mirrors the fear in my face. I don't know these people. It feels like they're not my people anymore. The smell of this air. It's not the smell of home. And no one smiles at me. Not a soul. Not the women who tug my emergency passport away from me and usher me through roughly. Not the porters whistling loudly and dragging mounds of bags behind them. No one knows what this moment means to me. And everything feels so big that it almost dwarfs me. The people are big. They tower over me. And I suddenly realise I miss the faces of Thailand. Their smiles, their petite bodies. Their language that I'd adopted as my own. And I don't know, after travelling all this way, if I actually belong here.

And outside, something else is waiting for me that I don't think I'm ready to face. My old life that wants to come rushing back at me in one huge tsunami. The faces, the voices, the memories of before. I don't know if I can go beyond this waiting area that separates me from them. I turn to Markus. "I can't do it. I can't. I can't go any further, Markus. Is there another way we can go out? I don't think I'm up to seeing everyone… I don't think I can deal with the media…"

I'm holding onto him tightly now. Shaking. Trying to slow my breath. Trying to train my heart to beat more gently in my chest. Wiping the sweat from my palms onto my clothes.

Markus is level-headed and patient. "Try to calm down. You made it through sixteen and a half years. And this is just the last episode. You'll get through it, Vanessa. I'm here."

"Okay, but I just need to sit down. Just for a few minutes to clear my head."

He finds us a seat. And while we sit there, he comforts me. He reassures me that I can do this and he'll never leave my side.

That's what he's been saying the entire journey. Those first few hours were so amazing for me. The aeroplane food looked strange. I was so excited, I got Markus to take pictures of it all with his camera. We had to stop off in Doha for four hours in transit and I was so cold, I put on three layers of socks and Markus's warm jersey. I shivered uncontrollably. He bought me hot Milo. We lay on a bench together, him trying to warm me with the heat of his body. None of it helped. My body only remembered the sweltering heat of Thailand. But it was also pure nervousness and fear causing me to shake. The journey was long. I was tired. But I couldn't sleep.

And then we board the next plane for South Africa and the anxiety creeps deep under my skin and spreads throughout me. Makes me feverish. Brings on sweats and a hammering heart that keep me awake. I'm desperate to pass out and wake up on another day that won't be so hard. That won't test me emotionally. I batter Markus with questions. First I want to know every half hour how far away we are. Then it's every fifteen minutes, ten minutes, five minutes. "I think you should stop asking me and just calm down," Markus says gently. But it only gets worse closer to our landing. When the plane begins its slow descent, then slams down onto the runway, I realise I'm home. *I am home*. The thought completely overwhelms me. The other passengers are filing out and all I can do is sit there, crying like a wreck, unable to tell Markus exactly how I feel.

It's stupid. But I'm scared. How can I tell him I won't get off because I don't want to see how old my mother's got since I left? Or I'm afraid to count how many more years of Felicia's life I've lost while she's become a young woman in my absence? Or that I'm dreading seeing Hilton and the kids without Melanie at his side? I can't.

So I force myself out of the plane and when my foot hits the ground, it takes me a moment to absorb this reality. *I'm actually standing on South African soil after all these years*. I'm so moved by this. I close my eyes and I breathe in the air. And the tears stream from the corners of my shut eyes because all these years, I've grieved as much for the loss of my country as I have for my family.

And now I'm sitting in the bustle of this massive airport, with all its levels and its flashing signs and hordes of travellers with their fancy suitcases on the escalators. And I'm wondering why I feel I don't fit in. Why, from the moment I've walked into this airport, it hasn't made me feel that I'm home. That sense of relief, that feeling of belonging, where is it? Where's the South African warmth I remember from all those years ago? Part of me wants to turn back now. It whispers doubt in my ear. Makes me want to return to that horrible life at Lard Yao just because I know it better. I know the smells of that place and the people and their language and their customs. And I realise that I'm out of place here because I've forgotten how to be South African. And I'll have to learn it again, from scratch.

I breathe deeply in and out of a brown paper bag Markus has given me on the plane. I've had a few minutes to gather my thoughts. But now he says, "Vanessa, we can't sit here for too long because the people are waiting for us. It's not going to get any better. This anxiety will build up until you pass through that door." So I don't think about it a moment longer. I stand up and we start walking.

And I hear Markus on the phone to Felicia a second later: "We're coming through now." And I can hear a mature voice on the other side saying, "Okay. Wow..." And I sense she's as scared as I am.

And as we near the doors, they see me through the glass. And they go berserk and start screaming, my family and friends – *"She's home! She's home!"* And it's so loud, it frightens me! But the doors part and I'm suddenly on the other side and people are screaming and crying and Felicia runs up to me and flings herself against me and I take her in my arms tight, so tight, almost suffocating her.

God! How long have I waited to hold my child like this in my arms? And I break down because she's here, her warm body bonded to mine. I can feel her heart racing in her chest and I want this moment to last forever. I never want to let go of her, ever. Because in this body of a teenager, I can still feel her childish frame of three years clinging to me in that prison, saying in her small voice, "Mommy, promise you'll come back soon." And I'm nodding and saying, "Yes, I promise Mommy will be home soon." And it hurts so much that it's taken me thirteen and a half years to keep that promise. And I hope she sees that even if it took me this long, at least I haven't broken it.

Standing behind Felicia is the outline of my mother. My shrunken mother with her older face. Gaunt, as though she's been eaten away over the years. So much pain and worry carved deep into the lines of her face. She looks confused, as though she's just been woken up from a deep sleep of many years and doesn't quite know where she is. And when she holds me, all she has are tears. No words. Words are empty. They can't explain more than sixteen years of separation from her child. They can't carry in them the meaning of a loss so hard to bear that she would set her house alight and try to burn herself alive in it. So when she cries softly, I hold her and I let her. Now we have more in common than we ever did. She's suffered from her love for me the same way I've suffered from my love for Felicia.

Aunty Rushda's eyes are red from crying. She throws her arms around me. I look at her face. She hasn't aged like my mom. She's always been the stronger of the two, and that's given my mom the courage to hold on. The crowd parts slightly and there, in the gap, stand three people, an incomplete family – Hilton, Lerell and Tatum, looking so wounded. Still in shock from their mother's death. And I'm living this moment I feared so much because Collette and Christine are there too, all of us standing, holding each other in a group, huddled in this blend of joy and sadness, our tears both for my freedom and for the loss of Melanie. And I'm bitter at the unfairness of this. For the first time in years when we are finally together again, one of us is still missing. And we'll never be complete without Melanie.

It all happens so fast after that. There's a camera in my face and Vanessa Govender of the eNews Channel is asking me questions, and I say something but I don't even know if it makes sense. And when she's done there's another layer of people to get through. More familiar faces and some I can't quite place. Elmarie is there. A stranger who heard my story and became my friend at the hardest time of my life in Lard Yao. She's visited me in jail and given Felicia her love and support here at home. And she's bursting with happiness as she hugs me. Pastor Pretorius from the Nazarene Church I attended in Eldorado Park has come here all the way from Cape Town. I thank him for all the letters he sent me in prison. And after he prays over my family and me, I feel that the strength he asks for enters me.

Every sense of mine is overloaded. This morning, I touch, taste, feel, hear, see in the brightest colours, the loudest sounds, the most intense emotions. I'm caught in a downpour but I allow it to soak me, to drench me, to start dissolving the pain of all these years I've been robbed of. I'd been afraid that when this moment came, I would break down, have a full-blown anxiety attack, because it's happened that way so many times. But I don't. My child is close to me. My mother is safe. My friends have not forgotten me. Markus has kept his promise of never leaving my side. My spirit is singing. My heart is awakened to this swell of love around me. I walk out into the morning light. Hear the hum of the city outside. There's a long road ahead for all of us. But thank God, I'm home. I'm finally home.

CHAPTER 26

A new life

There are many waiting cars lined up as we come out of the airport and I don't know which one to step into. There's a bit of shuffling and I feel torn because I want to give a piece of myself to everyone, but I can't right now. I'm hustled into Ivan's car. He, too, is a friend I made during my prison years and he's been very much a part of organising this return home. My mother and Aunty Rushda are travelling with me. But I'm a bit sad that Felicia and Markus are in the other car. I don't want my daughter to feel that I've abandoned her again, just moments after I've come back.

We hardly speak in the car at all. My mother is still crying. Aunty Rushda is unusually quiet. I'm car sick, which also gives me an excuse not to talk because I really have nothing to say. They may be my mother and my aunt but there's a real distance between us and Markus is really the only person I feel close to right now. My eyes are drawn outside and I'm mesmerised by what I see. Tall buildings seem to have sprung up all over. There's an old double-decker bus the colour of eggplant that I remember from years ago. But it's the only one of its kind I spot. The others are newer buses, splashed with bright paint and all sorts of advertising.

I look out for any places I recognise. But they all look unfamiliar to me. And when we drive through town, I'm shocked at how shabby, run-down and filthy the city looks. I can't believe it because we used to come here as kids. It was one of our favourite things to do. But the shops are shuttered and there's litter everywhere. And my family says the crime rate in town has gone up a lot over the years. There are millions of refugees from neighbouring countries like Zimbabwe, and many who can't make ends meet are living in abandoned buildings close to the city. All I can think is, if this is how much Jo'burg city has changed, imagine how many other things have too.

We arrive at Hilton's home in Sophiatown. It's big and comfortable. They've spent the last five months building an extension that I'll be staying in for now. We've all agreed that now that I'm back, Felicia shouldn't be uprooted. This is her family and she belongs in this home. The smell of delicious food is wafting from the kitchen. Melanie's family has prepared a feast for me although I don't know how much of it I'll be able to get down. While the women move in and out of the kitchen, I sit in the lounge quietly, Felicia on one side, Markus on the other.

I'm exhausted. But I'm also uncomfortable. I don't know what to say, who to talk to, how to respond to what everyone is saying. They all talk over each other and repeat the same thing: "I don't believe she's here"; "I can't believe it's really you"; "Thank God she's come back." And every now and then, someone cries or comes up to hug me again.

But it's difficult to express myself and tell them how I'm feeling. I don't want to be rude, but getting out of Lard Yao, through Immigration, onto that plane and landing here has drained me. All I want to do is have a hot bath, climb into bed and sleep – not just because I'm tired but because when I wake up, I'll know for sure this is not a dream and I really am back in South Africa. But they've planned this whole welcome-home lunch and I don't want to disappoint anyone. So I say a few words every now and then that I think are appropriate. And the rest of the time, I just sit back and watch.

What I can't stop doing, is caressing my daughter. I touch her at every opportunity. But I don't know what to say to her. Felicia and I – we're strangers to each other. But each time I touch her soft skin, I can't get over it – I can't believe this is my child. I really can't come to terms with it. She's so grown up. She speaks well, she has a mind of her own. She's independent and does everything for herself. And even though I've seen her a few times in prison after she left Lard Yao, in my mind she's still that three-year-old who was once so dependent on me.

Lunch is wonderful. There's roti, curry, a range of salads. They've made all my favourite food, but I can hardly touch it. After lunch, Collette tells me she, Melanie's family, Aunty Rushda and Ivan have planned a big party in a week's time. It'll be a joint Welcome Home Vanessa / Felicia's sixteenth birthday party. I hope I'm up to it. Collette's also decided to spoil me with a spa package that'll be done right here at home. I can expect a manicure, a pedicure and a full-body massage. I can't wait for it! Everyone's gone out of their way for me. Felicia's prepared my room. In it are twin beds on either side of the room where Markus and I will be sleeping. My room is packed with new clothes and it's full of gifts. Everyone sits around while I open them. They seem to have found the perfect presents for someone who's had very little for a very long time. I'm so overwhelmed that I have value in these people's eyes. I'm choked up at how special they make me feel.

But the highlight of that evening is my first hot bath in sixteen and a half years. And as the steam rises and I dip my foot in, I begin to cry. This is heaven! It makes me think of the women left behind. I remember so many nights when we sat up, speaking about what it would be like to sink our bodies into a warm, bubbly bath. And the tears come, because I can still see them, bodies pressed together, standing under a pipe punctured with a few holes, having their 15-second cold shower outside every morning. But as wonderful as the idea of a hot bath is, it's too hot for me. I'm used to ice-cold water on my body, so I have to add cold water to this bath to make it lukewarm.

And my bed! I love my bed with its marshmallow soft mattress, its puffy pillows and sheets that smell of clean. I sit on it and bounce a bit and I have a childlike feeling of being given a birthday present I was hoping so hard for but thought was way out of my reach. I pull the duvet cover over me and lie under it, and feel like I've been sandwiched in whipped cream. I haven't been able to cover myself for years while I slept in prison. And there's space. I can stretch my legs out and splay my arms and all this space is mine. I feel like a guest in a five-star hotel. I can't remember ever living this way. Or maybe I just didn't appreciate it as much the first time.

I'm not used to sleeping with the lights off because they burn all night in Lard Yao. But Felicia agrees she'll share the bed with me, which makes me less afraid of the dark. Markus climbs into the other bed. He wants to be close to me. I don't care that Felicia's a teenager and it's probably not cool to share a bed with her mom at this age. But I don't care. All I want to do is snuggle up to her and hold her in my arms. That night, I spend hours lying awake, just enjoying the comfort of the bed. I'm also running over the events of the last 24 hours, thinking of the flight, re-living the airport experience. Thinking of the others still stuck at Lard Yao.

The next morning I get up with severe body pains. It's going to be a while before I get used to sleeping on a bed again. I plan to have a hot shower but the water burns me, so I turn the hot water off completely and have a cold shower instead. I can't wait to go shopping, and Shoprite is the first store I head for. I spend three full hours in there, but Markus is very patient. I go through every aisle, I hone in on every shelf. I want to buy everything my eyes fall upon. I haven't seen peaches for sixteen and a half years. I want them. And I want avocados too. I'm so excited! I've dreamt and dreamt of all these things for so many years and now they're sitting here, right before my eyes and I can buy them myself! The only thing that shocks me is how expensive everything is. I can hardly believe that a loaf of bread now costs ten rand.

And just because I know I can now eat whenever I please, I raid the fridge round 1am that morning. I grab a blushing peach out of there and feel its fluffiness in my hand. I bite into it and it's ice-cold! The juice trickles down my chin and I take care to love every mouthful equally. I eat it down to the last fibres sprouting from the seed. It's wonderful! I take the whole bucket of peaches into my room, and Markus, who's got up to eat a peach with me at this time of the morning, shakes his head and says, "Why don't you put those back in the fridge?" And I say "No! What if the others finish them?"

"Then we'll go back to the shops and get some more."

And what he says makes perfect sense to me, but hording is a habit formed in prison, where we always hid things so they wouldn't get stolen. I'm also in the habit of eating everything down to the last crumb. I eat apples, core and all, not wasting even the tiniest bit, because in jail I never knew whether I'd ever have any again.

Otherwise, I don't eat much. In prison, I couldn't afford much food. I used to eat in the morning and at lunchtime. Because I gave an aerobics class at 3pm and went to shower afterwards, there was no time for supper. So sometimes, I'd quickly eat a piece of fruit and get back to the cell in time for lockdown at 5:30pm. Or else I'd go without any supper at all. When I first went to jail, there were nights when my stomach would claw with hunger. But because there was no money for food, I trained my body to get by on two meals a day. And that's why when we sit down to supper every evening now, I can hardly eat a thing. If I do, it makes me sick. I'm also still operating on prison time. I wake up at 3 or 4am in the morning and lie awake, thinking. Then I get tired and fall asleep at around 6am. And from the moment I open my eyes again, I'm dashing about, doing everything as quickly as I can. It's as though I'm still stuck in the prison routine where everything has to be done according to the clock.

I soon realise that it's important to have a full health check now that I'm back home. I've spent years sleeping almost on top of women with TB, leprosy and several other illnesses in Lard Yao. I go to Dr Marlin McKay's practice in Florida. He's polite, warm and well dressed and he does a thorough examination of me. And although I spend a nerve-wracking few days waiting for my test results, they're all clear. He tells me all I need to do is put on a bit of fat! But he also refers me to a psychologist to talk through my experience.

Soon after I get back home, Collette and Christine take me out to a restaurant. We chat for a while but it's such a struggle to relate to them. We're worlds apart and it saddens me because these two were more than friends to me. They were like my sisters, but now I have so little to talk to them about. They ask me if I'm alright to tell them about my time in prison and I say yes. But after a while, I get emotional and we have to talk about something else. I'm really interested in their lives though – in who they've married and what their husbands are like and how many children they have and what their jobs entail. And I see that they're happy and I'm so glad for them. But it also reminds me how far I've been left behind and how much lost time I have to make up for.

I've been so cut off from what's going on in the world that I don't know who's who. I know nothing about politics or sport or even who's running the government right now. Information about the outside world was kept from us in prison and I feel stupid when I hear other people discussing these things and I can't take part. Since I've been in jail, television hasn't been a part of my life, but when I get back, I'm glued to news programmes and I watch nothing else. If I can bring myself up to date with most things going on in the world, I know I won't feel so left out in company.

Technology is a battle on its own. I fight with my cellphone and laptop every day. Markus bought me a laptop and Felicia is showing me how to access the internet and send emails. In the Lard Yao computer room, the computers were so outdated they were still running on MS-Dos. So I have to get to grips with the internet and emails now. I leave my cellphone at home often because I haven't used any kind of phone for so long. And when I get my cellphone, I'm amazed that you can reach someone almost anywhere at any time even when you're on the move. But I get frustrated when my friend phones repeatedly and I cancel the call by pressing the wrong button. She explains patiently that there's a green button to pick up a call and a red one to drop it and then I start to get my head around it. But when someone promises to sms me, I'm completely puzzled. I soon learn that it's possible to send and receive text messages. I also sit at the computer all day, thinking that I have to respond to emails immediately as you would to a phone call, until Felicia tells me that I can do this at my leisure because even if I close the email programme and open it up again, the message will still be there.

There are even simpler things I struggle to remember. When I'm sick, I immediately self-medicate with any home remedy I can find because I'm just so used to it. I have to remind myself now that I'm back home that all I have to do is pick up the phone, make an appointment and get myself to the doctor when I'm ill. Sometimes I miss my friends, and when I see them and tell them this, they ask me why I didn't just call. And I tell the truth – I forgot there is such a thing as a cellphone. And if something's worrying me, I often shut myself up in my room and stay there for hours trying to solve it, without realising there are so many people around me who love me and would be only too happy to help.

But what I wrestle with most of all now that I'm back is the truth of what I've faced in Lard Yao. When you're locked into that prison system, the only thing you're focused on is your survival. Now, I'm on the outside looking in and I can truly see what prison life has done to me. And what I see hurts so much. One day when Melanie's mother is cooking some rice and she drains it and throws the water away, I say "Aunty Ellen, we drank that water. When I was pregnant, they told me it was good for me. I even made my Milo with that water." And she looks at me with pity.

And then, so many things suddenly flash through my mind – being told "sit on the ground every time an officer walks past; never look them in the eye." The water shortages when we bathed with one bowl of water and couldn't use the toilet. That picture of the girls with long hair sitting in a row of twelve chairs, in tears, while the officer slashed their locks in one fluid movement so they wouldn't waste water washing their long hair. I remember the intersexed woman whose skirt they undid and how they laughed at what was between her legs and took photos of her nakedness and made her cry. And I can't forget the blue face and purple lips of that Ukrainian girl wheeled out on a trolley after they said she'd hanged herself in solitary confinement.

I realise what they did to us in there – what they did to me.

How they turned me into a savage, only half human, bathing in a trough and eating food fit for animals and locking me in a cage every night. And everything I consider such a luxury today – the soft bed I sleep on and the good food I eat, the hot running water and the joy of contact with those I love – they all point to one thing: what a life of deprivation I led for sixteen and a half long years. And I can't believe I lived through it and I don't know how I ever got used to it. Lard Yao was nothing short of hell. And if I came out of that alive, I'm more than ready to take on this new life with all its challenges.

CHAPTER 27

Reintegration

I need to find work as soon as possible. I've only been home for two weeks, but I can't sit here doing nothing while Hilton's at work and the girls are at school. After I've done the cooking and a bit of cleaning, there's very little else to do. At Lard Yao, I was used to working long hours and I need to get back to doing something productive again.

Years ago, I met a South African man in the computer room during one of the United Nations visits to the prison. He immediately spotted me among the foreigners, came over and chatted to me in Afrikaans, asking me what I was planning to do when I got back home. I told him I was hoping to find a job at a non-governmental organisation or community upliftment programme. So he put me in touch with the director of one such NGO by the name of Jean. I immediately started writing to her and she wrote back to say she was keen to meet me.

Now that I'm back in the country, I decide to call Jean. We set up a time to meet and I take Collette with me. Jean is friendly, successful and more than prepared to help me. She promises that she'll put me through a reintegration programme if I decide to work for her. I'm especially interested in her projects that include prisoner furniture-building programmes and a number of other initiatives to help poor communities. Her work is spread throughout South Africa and it'll also give me a chance to travel and get to know this country of mine that's changed so much.

Jean takes me on almost immediately. I go through two weeks of orientation in December. And in January, she offers me a six-month contract. I'm going to have to balance all these aspects of my life carefully. I'm caring for three children and Hilton now. I've had to learn to cook again after not doing it for so long. And I'm trying to get to grips with technology so it doesn't hold me back in my work.

I start with a punishing schedule. I mostly travel around the country giving talks about my life in prison. At other times, I go into local prisons and try to encourage the inmates to make something of their lives. Once they've heard my story, they realise that prison life in South Africa is difficult but it could be so much harder. I'm hardly ever at home. I'm either on a plane to Cape Town, Durban or some remote area to open a project or speak at events. Otherwise, I'm running between these projects to make sure they're running smoothly. Jean also asks me to start recording my story for the purposes of a book and I spend weeks writing a life skills programme dedicated to empowering women.

From January to June 2011, my life becomes a tornado. I whip in and out of the house. My friends hardly see me. I slap meals together in advance and freeze them so no one goes hungry. I live past Felicia, who's been waiting so many years to see me, but now spends about as much time with me as she did when I was locked up. I can't sleep, so I'm constantly tired during the day. And there are some days when I don't want to stand in front of people and share my prison experience because talking about it is just too painful. But my life never slows down. It only gets worse over the months, this feeling of being kicked about like a football.

I end up pushing myself so hard that by the time I get to Cape Town to speak at a conference in June, I'm so burnt out that I'm rushed to Intensive Care. Jean is in Cape Town but she doesn't bother visiting me. When I'm discharged, I stay with my aunt in Kraaifontein. She takes care of me while I recover. One day while we're chatting, she tells me about how my grandfather died. And without meaning it, she carelessly says in passing, "you know, you were the cause of Papa's death." She explains how they tried to keep my arrest a secret from him, but he read an article in the *You* magazine, immediately began having chest pains, was rushed to hospital and died of a heart attack shortly afterwards.

This news shakes me so badly that all my symptoms suddenly return. I have terrible shortness of breath. I'm sweating. I have to rush outside to get some air. And I'm pacing up and down on the pavement while my aunt watches. I ask her to please take me to a doctor because I know how this will end. I'm rushed to the doctor who treats me and prescribes medication to relieve my stress. I feel sorry for my aunt because I know that what she told me was never meant to hurt me. But the rest of the family is quite hard on her, blaming her for this setback in my health. I stay in Cape Town and only go back to Jo'burg once I've fully recovered.

Once I'm feeling better, I return to work. But Jean and I have started to disagree on many things. I feel she wants to control me and I won't allow her to do this. We argue about the life skills programme I've designed, about the recordings for my book and why she won't give me a raise when I'm doing much more than my job requires. This no longer feels right to me. I thank her for her efforts to reintegrate me and then I leave. But this job has taken its toll on the most important relationship in my life – my relationship with my daughter – and I can't let it go on like this.

Felicia is angry with me. We've made no progress in moving forward as mother and daughter because I've been travelling so much. And our relationship is strange to say the least. When I sit down and try to talk to her, she laughs. I don't know her. I don't feel like her mother. And if I see her doing something wrong, I don't even know if I have the right to interfere and tell her what to do.

On the occasions when I do, she reacts so badly. She's upset with me for shouting at her, speaking aggressively as though she's a naughty child. And I don't mean to be this way. These are my "prison manners" – this terrible habit I have of raising my voice, always speaking loudly and firmly so that no one takes advantage of me. I haven't really spoken softly for many years. And sometimes the problem is what I say. So when she comes to me in a crisis, I encourage her to stand her ground because that's part of what I've had to learn to do, to survive in jail.

And she sees this as some kind of superhuman strength I'm showing off that helps me to get over my problems. She keeps on saying, "I'm not like you. I'm not as strong as you!" And I wish I could tell her how weak I often feel inside. Felicia and I fight all the time. She walks away from me. I know I'm sometimes insensitive but I tell Felicia one day in the most sincere way I can, "Fifi, I'm trying to be a mother. I just don't know how." And she tells me to stop making excuses.

All I can think is that this child has no idea where I'm coming from. She has no idea what I've gone through or how much I'm struggling. And then I realise, exactly the same applies to me. Part of her anger has to do with this imaginary picture of me she's built up in her mind. "Supermodel Supermom Vanessa." Because she never gets to know me when she's growing up, she fills in all the blanks with this image of a quiet, gentle, perfect mother who can fulfil all her needs. And I come back just the opposite – unsure of myself, loud, flawed, full of pain from my past.

Each of us knows the other has suffered. We just don't know how to tell each other. Felicia never shares what she went through waiting for a day called "soon" when I would come back home and we'd be a family again. And I've never told her about the horrors of prison life because I don't want to scar my child with those stories. We go for counselling together but she asks to speak to the counsellor alone and I do the same. So that wall between us never comes down. It just seems to get one brick thicker every day.

It doesn't help that she's still mourning Melanie. And she can't even express those feelings because she wants to become the glue that Melanie was, holding this family together. They're all struggling. Hilton is wilting from his grief. He wants to get rid of all traces of Melanie in the house as though she never lived here – photos, cards, all reminders of her are pulled off shelves and walls and hidden away. One day, Hilton walks into the lounge and the kids are watching a home video of Melanie and he's somehow so shocked to see the pictures of the woman he loved that he walks out in tears. And only when I've sat down with him for hours that night and we've talked it through, does he see that Melanie will never leave us. The next day, I restore all her pictures to their rightful place. The children seem relieved that they no longer have to hide this yearning for their mother and pretend they're over her death.

There's another factor that's weighing heavily on Felicia's relationship with me. Felix, her father, the one individual I dreaded seeing the most, suddenly re-appears in Felicia's life. The last time I saw him was in prison before her birth and for more than sixteen years he's pretended she doesn't exist. Some time after Melanie's death, he comes to the house and tells Hilton he wants to be a part of Felicia's life. But then he disappears again, and when Felix comes back a second time, Hilton tells him he's not welcome in their home anymore.

We're all trying to shield Felicia from the disappointment of a father who may not live up to his promises, just like he's done in the past. He's full of excuses as to why he never looked after Felicia when I was in jail. He says he went through a difficult time, no one wanted to help him after I was arrested and he even went back to Mozambique to clear his head. But in truth, he's moved on with his life completely since then. Eventually, after resisting it for a long time, I let Felicia have her way and see him. It's her right – he is her father, after all. And even though I've seen him try to drive a wedge between my daughter and me, I have to believe that she'll see the truth for herself one day.

Months pass and I stop and take stock of what I've achieved. When I left Lard Yao to come home, I thought it was the small challenges of life that would slow me down and prevent me from becoming a part of this society again. But it's not learning who's in government or getting to know the country's sporting champions that's a problem. It's not taking driving lessons that fray my nerves or finding a job that's been so difficult. It's not even using phones and computers that makes me want to tear my hair out.

The toughest part of reintegration is welding my life with the lives of the people I love. Smashing down the walls that stop us from reaching one another. Trying to weave this picture so that all our lives are knotted together firmly, and I'm in the midst of them, not feeling like an outsider anymore.

The only positive thing I have to hold onto right now is my relationship with Markus. We both enjoy my freedom so much because I can now phone him, text him, message him on Facebook, Skype him at almost any time of the day. He phones me and we speak every day. He advises me on any work or legal matter, taking his time to explain it without making me feel stupid. And when things get difficult with Felicia and my emotions spin out of control, it's only the sound of his voice on the other end that brings me back into balance.

Because Markus holds this big position of CEO at his German software firm, he can't visit me too often. But after he accompanies me home, he leaves and comes back with his son, Nicholas, in December to visit us. It turns out to be a wonderful family holiday, and it seems Felicia and Nick are almost starting to see themselves as brother and sister although there's still a language barrier.

But the coming and going of Markus is challenging. Each time he leaves, it's hard for the both of us. I sense sometimes that he's afraid he'll lose me while he's away. And I miss him so much, because speaking to this image of him on Skype or hearing his voice on the phone just isn't enough anymore. It's not the same as having him here with me, talking to me, helping me, touching me. Without him here, I'm constantly afraid I'll make the wrong decisions. The one stupid mistake I made in my life, carrying those books as a favour to Jackson, has ruined me, so I no longer trust the decisions I make. I wish Markus was close by.

There's just one thing about our arrangement that worries me. He says quite openly, all the time, "I'm going to take you away from South Africa," and he means it. He wants me to marry him and settle down in Germany. But I'm not ready to go. I've waited years to get back home, to live in my country and walk in its streets and be with my people. And I'm not ready to pull myself away from this attachment I have to South Africa. I simply need more time to readjust. But maybe it's difficult for Markus to see this after waiting for me for so long.

He suggests I start learning German and apply for a visa to go to Germany to see what it's like there and start making plans for a wedding. But talking of the future away from the home and country I have just found panics me. I have a daughter here who doesn't know me. We're trying to build a relationship out of nothing and this takes time. Hilton and the girls also need me now. I may never have had a chance to say a proper thank you to Melanie, but this is the only way I can do it now that she's gone – try to fill her shoes the way she filled mine. Most of all, I know that somewhere in Lard Yao, I lost Vanessa, and right now I'm desperately trying to find her.

At first, I feel obligated to go along with Markus's suggestions after all he's done for me. He's shown me such kindness and care. I don't want to disappoint him. But when I ask in passing if he wouldn't mind settling in South Africa instead, because he once suggested it as a possibility, he seems offended by my question. In his mind, I'm refusing to go to Germany. I try to make him see it from my point of view. But he sees my *not yet* as a *no* and this leads to many arguments. Markus gets upset. Says he misses the woman in prison. But he doesn't understand that the woman in prison never had to juggle all these things – a grief-stricken household, three children and a demanding job.

And when he comes to visit me in December and March, there are many things I see about him for the first time that don't sit well with me. He's an organiser. He plans everything down to the last detail. There's no room to be flexible or adaptable. And I tell him not to be so uptight, because for the last two decades almost, I've been living strictly by rules, by the clock, by the calendar in Lard Yao, and I don't want to live like this anymore. Then Markus suggests we go away to Mauritius in June for two weeks.

The island is pure perfection. It's the most romantic place to get married. But even in the beauty of that setting, I'm not at ease with the idea of commitment. I gather that he's come here, planning to have a wedding on the island. But I feel like I need more time to readapt to my old life. I've been suffering from too many emotional setbacks since my return. Markus is visibly upset by my answer and seems to take it as a rejection.

When we get back to South Africa, he stays on for a week although he's threatened to leave earlier. He has a bag with him. And I ask him what's in it. But he won't say. He clutches it like a wounded animal and I can see the hurt in his eyes. And I'm so sorry I've done this to him because he's a decent man. A loving, giving man who's sacrificed so much for me. And he opens the bag and it's full of us. Of every card, every letter, every little trace of all his visits to the prison. And there's nothing more to say. This is how Markus breaks up with me. And he leaves a slightly hunched man, still unable to believe that after all he did for me, he leaves with nothing. And I'm sad too, because all I have of him are these paper souvenirs that could never ever sum up the depth of his love for me.

CHAPTER 28

Into the future

I am 40 years old.

It's the morning of 18 December 2012. More than two years since I stepped out of Lard Yao to freedom. I expect Felicia and the girls to come flooding into my bedroom at any moment now with their cries of "Happy Birthday!" They go out of their way to make my birthdays special because we've missed so many together. But today, I'm not in the mood for it. I just want to slither back under these covers, close my eyes and dream about anything but how old I am.

Forty years. Four decades. Everyone else wants to celebrate this birthday of mine. "It's a milestone!" they say. But all I want to do today is grieve the lost years. Because just a moment ago, I was 22 years old, fresh faced, standing on the brink of my exciting life. But it vanished before me so quickly, so cruelly and I don't know how to make up the lost time. There's no way of pretending that I haven't lost a big, fat chunk of my life. I look at those around me – Collette, Christine, Hilton. They've accomplished so much in the years I was gone, and what have I got to show for all that time? Not a thing. Not a house or a vehicle or a marriage or a career. I feel like a car-crash victim learning to walk again. Everyone urges me to take baby steps. But all I want to do is leap forward because the clock never stops ticking and I want what everyone else has.

My age starts to upset me so much that I go to talk to my pastor about it. "I can't handle it. It's making me sick! What does a person do at 40? Where do I start when I have nothing?" He can see I'm anxious, angry, frustrated. He calmly says, "Vanessa, you've accomplished so much in this short time that many others have struggled to do over several years. Talk to other people about the difficulties of their lives. People who've stayed here and lost none of the time you did. So many are trying to come to terms with broken relationships, failed marriages, alienated children, unemployment, financial strain, mistakes they've made in those years. When you feel like you want to give up, remember that you've survived a tough situation that many others didn't. And there has to be a reason for that."

Since I've come back, I've been searching for that reason. I know I could've died in prison. I was on the verge of it. Why was I saved? And once I find out, what am I supposed to do with that information? I take my pastor's advice. I talk to people. I hear their stories. I see how bruised they are by the horrors life pelts them with. And more and more, my heart is being drawn to those people. My eyes are suddenly opened to how many sad souls there are around me. People nursing broken hearts and fear. People who've suffered trauma and never got over it. People who are yearning for any love they can get – even the type that leaves them with black eyes and broken bones. And this desire begins to stir in me to listen to them and try to help them.

This is not the first time I've had this feeling, although in the past, the urge hasn't been this strong. For years at Lard Yao, women came to me and spoke openly about their problems. There were Thais and foreigners among them. Women who held different religious beliefs to mine. But there was a point where we connected because life at Lard Yao was really a sisterhood. All of us scarred, chained, praying for freedom, wishing for some sliver of happiness to enter our empty lives. And those who came to me would speak and I'd offer them the best advice I could and it would give them some relief. There were some who'd come to chat for just a few minutes, others who'd speak to me every day for months and come back saying, "Thank you. You've helped me a lot." And it was completely informal, but I began to see I have a heart for this. That I can't witness another human being's suffering and turn away from it. People have come to me at the lowest point of their lives and I've done my best to uplift them, to help them change their situations or their attitude to those situations. And this has given me so much joy. I've watched women with broken wings rise and fly – women you wouldn't believe are prisoners anymore. They dig deep and they find something inside themselves – a spark that gives way to a bonfire. And it fuels them to go on every day, to survive, never to give up until they're standing at Lard Yao's doors waiting to walk out as free women.

The most powerful thing I can give them is the reality that I've suffered like them. I know how it feels. I lay on that hospital bed for months baiting death and in the moment when I came closest to it, that was when I knew I wanted to live. I had to live. There was a purpose for my life – I wasn't born for nothing. And here, in South Africa right now, I see more of those people. Their faces are different, but the hurt in their eyes is the same. I see pain in this society like I saw it in Lard Yao, and I suddenly know that this is why I survived. I survived to show others they can do the same.

It's not that my ghosts don't haunt me. There are days when I wake up and I say, "Sixteen and a half years." And those words are enough to lay me flat in my bed for the rest of the day because that timeframe is just too enormous for me to understand. When I go back and read the letters that my mother sent to me in prison, I go limp with sadness. I struggle to function for days afterwards. Fear and anxiety still knock on my door often. And sometimes, I open it to them.

There are silly little things that'll always affect me. Whenever someone uses the phrase "One moment, please," I can almost scream. That was the last thing said to me at the airport before I was sucked into the system that would steal so many years of my life. I also remember standing at the airport with Markus as we got ready to board our plane to Mauritius, and the stabbing pain I felt in my chest when they searched my bags, as though it was going to happen to me all over again. It makes no sense, but the memory of what I suffered never goes away. I'm learning to deal with it a little better every day.

I've also learnt that you choose what you hold onto and what you get rid of. Sometimes I'm asked why I feel no hatred or bitterness towards those who did this to me, or the Thais who locked me up without giving me a fair hearing. And I try to explain that it wasn't always like this. From the time of my arrest in Bangkok to the time I almost died in hospital, I fought the biggest battle. Anger and bitterness, black and smoking like lit coal, raged inside me. I hated with all my heart. I hated the people who did this to me. I hated Felix for never coming to rescue me or look after our child. I hated the system that chose to be blind to my innocence. And I hated Lard Yao with every cell in my body.

Even when I came back and Felix saw what a bitter human being prison had made me, he asked me, "What's going to make you happy, Vanessa?" And I said, "It'll make me happy to see you suffer." It outraged me that he never once asked me what it was like in prison, how I survived all those years on my own without his support. And when he told me the suffering I wished on him was cruel, I said, "But I mean it, Felix. I mean it from the bottom of my heart. You were in the free world. You could help yourself. My hands were cut off. I couldn't help myself." And he stared at me, but there was no hint of understanding in his eyes.

But one day, I wake up and it's 2013 already. And I realise, I've been fighting for so long. These fights have ended in major setbacks that have almost crippled me in prison and since I've come back. And every time I fight, the anger, the pain, the suffering return and fester inside me. I might as well be caught in that sixteen-and-a-half-year time warp again because that's the way I feel when I'm fighting, even though I've left that life behind. I remind myself that I nearly went insane fighting for my emotional survival in Lard Yao. I was nearly destroyed by hatred and bitterness. They kill you slowly without you realising it, and to uproot them can almost become impossible.

So I make up my mind that I'll never let anger, bitterness or hatred take over again. They are too powerful once you let them in. The only thing more powerful than them is forgiveness. Because forgiveness is the tool you use to cut these negative emotions away. And once you've freed yourself from them, you've also freed yourself from the power that certain people in your life have always had over you. And it makes those people powerless too.

I've had to pray hard for forgiveness. It doesn't come as easily as these destructive emotions. But now that I have it, I feel a release. It's a slashing of ropes that have bound me tightly for all this time, left marks on me. And now that they're lying in a loose pile at my feet, I have real freedom. I can think about me. About my needs and my success and how I intend to go forward with my life.

And this is how I do it. I go out there on my own and I start talking about my pain. I tell my story to anyone who'll listen. I speak at churches, conferences, events. I'm interviewed on radio and TV. Magazines talk to me about my experience. And each time I share my story, I come alive and it feels like I'm telling it for the first time. And afterwards, there are always a few people who trickle forward, their faces flooded with tears. And they share their story with me. "I've just found out I'm HIV positive" or "my father abused me when I was growing up" or "I've just got divorced and I don't know if I can live without my wife" or "I found out last week my husband's cheating on me."

And I want to throw my arms around them for having the courage to share this, to take their pain and turn it into words because I know that's never an easy thing to do. But what heartens me most is what they say before they leave. "I wanted to give up. I'd lost hope, but if you can go on hoping after what you've been through, I can go on too."

One day, a church minister phones me and says, "I was about to commit suicide the day you were interviewed on radio. And something you said stopped me and that's why I'm still alive and I want to thank you for that." My heart is so full that I cry. Because I know that this is part of being human. We're all longing for hope. We all need to feel that this life we're living is worthwhile and important to someone. And without that hope, the whole journey is pointless. I begin to feel that I've touched some lives and those people have had their hope restored. But no one really knows what this has done for me. Each time I tell my story, I'm healing. I feel the wound closing, a scab starting to form over it. And I think, maybe I've found my purpose in life and my healing in the same place.

Sometimes I still wonder about the reason I ended up in prison. I've spent years asking why it happened to me. But that's really a pointless question now because it happened and that's the reality. And all that matters today is how I deal with it. Lard Yao was many things to me. It was a brutal teacher of the kind of lessons you only learn from hardship. And it was the most unflattering mirror. When I stood in front of it, I saw no beauty. I saw all my flaws, all my weaknesses. I saw a frail, hopeless young woman staring back at me. And I worked on her, took her apart and re-moulded her, until I found the strength in her. And over the years, after I'd hated her for a long time, she slowly became someone I grew to like. Someone who kept her humanity even though this prison tried to take it from her. And when I looked in that mirror for the last time, on my way out, I saw strength and determination and courage.

Felicia and I are now on a new path. I feel like we've brought in a demolition gang and managed to knock down huge portions of that massive wall that almost stopped us from being the mother and daughter team we were always meant to be. I recall a time when we fought so much, and she confessed she had no respect for me. As much as her words cut me, they also made me realise that when I came back, I was so full of guilt from being an absent mother that I gave in too easily to her demands. Everything she wished for, anything she wanted that was within my reach, I let her have. But that's changed now and she understands why.

My daughter's also taught me a big lesson about promises. "You can do anything to me, but don't break a promise. When I give my word, I honour it. I never break a promise," she often says, sounding so much older than her 18 years. But I never understood what she meant until I started piecing it all together. I didn't know the careless promise I made in prison would come back to haunt me this way. *"Mommy will be back soon, Felicia."*

When I got back from prison, I sat going through all the letters I'd sent her over the years. And there are some really childish ones – my drawings of Felicia and me, two stick figures playing games outside. And there's always the same message scribbled at the bottom: "Mommy will be home soon." I remember Melanie telling me that Felicia had such an outburst one day and she shouted, "I'm sick of hearing this word *soon*! Stop saying that! She said she's coming back soon, but she lied to me!"

It took too many years, but soon's finally come. And I hope Felicia will begin to see that what I said to her the day she left Lard Yao was the only thing I could say in that impossible situation I was caught in. When I knew she was seconds away from being ripped away from me and taken to an orphanage if she didn't leave with Melanie, I had to say something to make her go – but it had to be something that would leave her with some shred of hope too, so it didn't feel like we were going to be apart forever. I said the only thing that sounded reassuring in the moment. And I hope that, in time, she'll believe that I never meant to lie to her.

These days, the two of us are slowly finding a window into each other's souls and we're happy with what we see inside. I've made peace with the fact that Felix is part of my daughter's life. I have to respect Felicia's choice to spend time with him. Having my own friends I can talk to, share the pain of my story with, and feel that they're prepared to take it on themselves at times, makes my journey so much easier.

Sometimes, though, I still wonder whether I'll ever know who decided that I should be the one to carry those drugs and take the fall for it. I have a strong suspicion that it may have been someone close to me. But without proof, I can't accuse anyone of this crime. And even if I did manage to lay my hands on that evidence, it wouldn't bring back sixteen and a half years of my life.

But what it shows is how one decision, the actions of a single person, can impact on so many lives so radically over a number of years. It changed my life, the lives of my family members and friends.

It resulted in separation, attempted suicide, death. It ruptured families and created new ones. But it also drew friendship and love from across the globe. It brought the compassion of volunteers and missionaries from the United States and the Philippines to my door. It broke the hearts of two men as far away as Germany and Norway, who still consider themselves my friends. These are the threads of the rich tapestry that have become my life. Threads that reach out over continents and seas and span many years. And maybe Felicia is right. Perhaps there is a season for everything, including the people who move in and out of our lives. They come and go as we need them.

I still write to some of the inmates at Lard Yao because I know how lonely it can get in there and how any letters they receive they treat like gold. I'm grateful that my prayer for the foreigners to flow out of the gates of Lard Yao in their numbers was answered. Soon after I left, many were released, including several South Africans and Ghanaians.

For now, I choose not to dwell on the past. When Lard Yao enters my mind, I try to think only about the lessons I've learnt and the women in there I shared many years of friendship with. Wherever we are in the world, those bonds stretch to touch us all. Somehow, even in our new lives, we are never without one another. And whenever we talk or send each other letters, the theme is always the same. We look at life differently, almost through the eyes of children. We find joy in the simplest things – sunsets and stars, dripping peaches and warm bed sheets. And we never forget to mention what a miracle it is to be alive, surrounded by our families who love us.

I cannot help but feel blessed to be back here in my own country, to witness my daughter making the leap from her teenage years to womanhood, and watch my mom growing old without worry. I feel privileged to pay tribute to Melanie by walking in her footsteps and trying to be a mother to her daughters. And each time I step out onto the street, go anywhere I want, eat and drink whatever I like, that's when I feel pure excitement at the tang of freedom in the air and the thought that I now have a second chance at everything.

I feel a lurch in my tummy. Exactly what I felt as the plane left Bangkok Airport and the sky sucked us upwards towards it and I felt my body and spirit rising high, bursting through the clouds, soaring above them.

There was a tradition we used to have at Lard Yao that when the day dawns for one of us to go free, we hold each other tight, we say our goodbyes and we shed our tears. But once our feet touch that threshold – once we are standing at the portal to our freedom – we push the door open hard and we go forward with determination. We may hear the voices of the people we love behind us, but as tempting as it is to turn around for one last glance, we never, ever look back. We look only to the future. We look to the lives ahead of us. We look to freedom and love and success and all the blessings those left behind are wishing on us. And if leaving Lard Yao teaches you one thing, it's to take that with you into the world.

Afterword

It is December 2011 and the footage of South African Nolubabalo Nobanda unfurling her lengthy dreadlocks to reveal the cache of cocaine within hits televisions screens around the world. Arrested at Bangkok International, she comes clean before the cameras in the presence of Thai police who take their war on drugs very seriously. At eNCA, the 24-hour news channel where I anchor Afternoon News, we are scrambling to find a window into how Nobanda must be feeling in these moments and what she faces in the days ahead. There are few people better placed to answer these questions than former South African Miss SA semi-finalist, Vanessa Goosen.

Goosen carries within her an intimate portrait of Thai prison life. It is clear that all those who have had a taste of this bear the signs of it in one form or another, long after they have left. For Goosen, that has taken the form of flashbacks, anxiety attacks and intermittent periods of depression since she returned home on 5 November 2010. Aside from the challenge of reintegrating into society, the question will always remain in the minds of others as to whether she knowingly tried to carry heroin out of Thailand all those years ago or whether she was indeed duped into doing it, as she claims. I ask Goosen during the lengthy televised interview we broadcast on eNCA shortly after Nobanda's arrest, "How do we know you're not lying when you deny knowing about the drugs in the books you were carrying?" Goosen's answer is that anyone who chooses to believe in her guilt has the right to do so because it is only natural to assume the worst of anyone when we are talking about the sensitive issue of drugs.

This interview becomes the basis of the book that I will begin writing almost a year later. The words on the page begin to materialise at a time when many more South Africans are being arrested and jailed for drug trafficking worldwide. In countries like Brazil, Peru, Indonesia and even Mauritius, we are earning the reputation as a nation of smugglers, nurtured by the growth of our country as a major transit point for trafficking. There are almost a thousand South Africans languishing in overseas jails, charged with drug trafficking. The Department of International Relations suggests this figure may be even higher, since many of our nationals arrested overseas choose not to have their embassies or families notified of their arrest.

For those arrested in Thailand, aside from the poor living conditions inside prisons, what may be the biggest adjustment to Thai prison life is the cultural shift that has to occur with foreign inmates – learning a new language, adapting to the food, sleeping on the floor packed like sardines, staving off disease, bathing with a few bowls of water from a trough, growing accustomed to body searches. But that does not take into account what may be the biggest issue, certainly for foreign female prisoners shut up in overseas jails. For Goosen and other foreign inmates, the vast distance and separation from their families, especially their children, sets them apart from the Thai prisoners who are able to enjoy regular visits from their families and friends.

Foreign inmates are limited to very few visits a year from their loved ones because travel to Thailand is so expensive. There have also been periods when Lard Yao officials would limit a foreign visitor to one visitation of half an hour in the period of a month, which would be a waste of the money funnelled into a plane ticket and accommodation. Many family members would choose to write letters to the prisoners instead, in case the officials barred them access on a whim. As time wore on, Goosen points out that the nature of visits changed too. They were shorter and took place in rooms where prisoners and their visitors sat far apart and could not see one another clearly or had to shout across many other prisoners to be heard. She describes this as traumatic, especially for the mothers among them who longed for closer contact with their children.

Goosen maintains, as she did in a 2006 letter to officials on behalf of all the South Africans incarcerated at Lard Yao, that these women have never asked the South African government for a reduction of their sentences should they be brought back home, as happens with the British and American judicial systems. What they did ask for was to be transferred home to serve out their sentences closer to their families, despite what many may describe as the deplorable conditions of our own jails. The injustice of this separation is perhaps best borne out in the case of Tessa Beetge, a drug mule and mother of two teenage girls who is serving out her eight-year sentence in a Brazilian jail far away from her family, while the convicted mastermind behind the operation, the former State Security Minister's ex-wife, Sheryl Cwele, has been jailed in South Africa where she will likely receive regular visits from her relatives. Following Cwele's conviction, Beetge's parents have asked Brazilian President Dilma Roussef to pardon their daughter. They say her children, aged 13 and 15, are yearning to be reunited with their mother whom they have not seen for four years.

This has fuelled anger among the families of those being held overseas, especially since South Africa's prisoner transfer treaty with Thailand seemed almost on the verge of being ratified during former president Nelson Mandela's tenure. Subsequent to that, there have been two changes of administration and both have done very little to advance the finalisation of this agreement. South Africa has adopted the stance that it will not interfere with the legal processes of another country where its own citizens are alleged to have committed a crime.

According to some, Thailand's justice system stands up to scrutiny. Douglas Gibson, former South African ambassador to

Thailand, who spent much of his early days as ambassador visiting prisons, says that the country's justice system is "respectable"in so far as judges seek to carry out the law as stipulated in Thailand's Constitution. But there are aspects of the Thai justice system that I believe must be called into question. How is it that following the suspect's arrest, no further investigation is done in many of these cases, especially those where mitigating circumstances may apply? Is it fair that Goosen and others have been tried in a language they do not understand and are often represented by apprentice lawyers who are poorly paid and have little court experience? Why are the accused compelled to sign confessions in Thai and refused a translation into their own language before they sign it? And can it be right that suspects are advised to plead guilty under duress so as to avoid the death sentence?

It is clear that Thailand treats drug-related charges with a great deal of seriousness. But to understand why, we must also zoom out to the wider context. High drug addiction rates in Thailand have prompted officials to announce a merciless clampdown on drug trafficking and use in the last few years. Thai police revealed in 2011 that one in every six Thai citizens was a methamphetamine user, and over a million of them would have used drugs in the space of just a year. The last time the Thai state effected this kind of crackdown was in 2003. Approximately 2 800 people were killed in the space of three months – and many of them are thought to have had nothing to do with the drug trade at all.

Clearly, the problem is widespread enough to demand an extreme official response, which should lead us to a greater understanding of how the traffickers themselves are viewed by the Thai justice system that seeks to make an example, even of the innocent. According to Amnesty International, the last executions (performed by lethal injection, which has replaced death by firing squad), took place in 2009, when two Thai men convicted of drug trafficking were put to death, reportedly an hour after they were informed that they were to be executed. But more often than not, in the case of foreign drug mules especially, death sentences are commuted to life and then reduced bit by bit through amnesties or pardons.

Perhaps the initial death sentence or life imprisonment is a scare tactic more than anything else. But it appears to have the desired effect. Goosen says that the threat of imminent death was very real to her when she was on death row, especially after she watched the clip on television of a man's execution. She tells of how, shortly after she arrived at Lard Yao, she was told the story of an older woman from a few years back who had been called into the office to speak to her family, offered a last meal of her choice and had her footprint taken. Goosen dreaded the day when she would face this. "Once they ask to take your footprint," she says, "you must know it's the end."

It appears that the length of sentences handed down may also differ according to whether or not a transfer agreement exists between the prisoner's country and Thailand. On the same day that Goosen received a life sentence for trafficking 1.7 kilograms of heroin, an American woman was given eight years in prison for carrying 15 kilograms of heroin into the country. No reason was given for the discrepancy. For a long time now, the South African government has believed that postponing the signing of the transfer treaty would act as a deterrent to potential drug mules. As journalist Karyn Maughan points out, in 1997, "former Deputy Foreign Minister Aziz Pahad was quoted as saying such agreements would 'send the wrong signal' and encourage other South Africans to get involved in carrying drugs." But in retrospect, we can argue that government's decision not to ratify the extradition treaty has done almost nothing to stem the steady stream of South Africans entering the drug mule trade.

It is interesting that our country also chooses to pay for the upkeep of approximately 7 000 foreigners who are either convicts or awaiting trial in our prisons. It is believed to be spending more than R100 million a year expatriating the rest to their mother countries. But it also refuses to extradite any foreigners who, although convicted in South Africa, will face the death sentence in their own countries if returned there. A case in point is that of convicted Nigerian terrorist, Henry Okah, whose activities led to the deaths of innocent civilians. By contrast, nothing could be done to save the life of South African Janice Linden, executed for drug trafficking by lethal injection in China in 2010.

Drugs are indeed an emotive issue. We cannot for a minute downplay the harm they cause to many societies, including our own. It is natural for ordinary people, whose lives are affected daily by the use of drugs and the influx of them into our country, to feel extreme anger over the destruction of innocent lives that is wrought by the greed of a few. But how many drug kingpins who drive the operations are sitting behind bars compared with the drug mules themselves, who are often pawns in a much bigger game that extends across borders and covers large tracts of the globe? There are those, particularly young men from the developed world, who may choose to carry drugs out of boredom, greed and bravado. But for Africa's drug mules, the reality appears to be quite different.

These mules usually fit a stereotype – they are individuals who have fallen on hard times and are desperate to find a quick and substantial source of income. Many are single or divorced women and men, unable to find work or support their families. And once offered this opportunity by the member of a syndicate, they begin to view this as a crime they will knowingly commit once off, just to get them back on their feet. This is a naïve view at best, because we are aware that despite carrying what we know to be a very expensive illegal substance, mules are often paid only a few thousand rand for risking their freedom. Many are unaware that they will be used as decoys – sacrificial lambs carrying small amounts of drugs who are somehow marked as they enter the airports, so that other smugglers on the same flights carrying larger quantities can pass through security unhindered. Nobanda's confession suggests that this is what happened to her. The alleged corruption often associated with Thai customs officials suggests they might well be open to allowing a few drug traffickers to pass through the net so they are assured of at least one arrest that makes the headlines.

Ultimately, this leaves us with the question that Goosen's lawyer raises in the book – whether the punishment fits the crime, regardless of whether the prisoner is guilty or not. The high crime rate in our country may prompt many to believe that the hardship you have read of in this book is a just and deserving punishment for those who break the law and dabble in drugs. Morally, there is nothing incorrect with that argument. But there is a human element to this that many of us will struggle with.

Gibson puts its rather eloquently himself when he says he is torn by the lawyer in him, who has practised this profession for over forty years, and the humanitarian in him who visits these women in jail and comes face-to-face with their pain.

"Intellectually, I think of what these people have done – the damage they do to other people. If my child became an addict, went to jail or committed suicide as a result of drug use, I'd want heavy penalties so that people learn. But when you deal with the individual people, then it becomes a little different. I'm a father, I have daughters and I feel so sorry when I speak to these young women. They cry when they tell me their story and I find myself crying too."

Ultimately, the intention of this book is two-pronged. It is the exorcism of the pain of Vanessa Goosen, caught up in this system as a young woman who lost many years of her life along the way. But it is also to remember those like Nolubabalo Nobanda, who will only re-enter our society when she is close to being a middle-aged woman. We as South Africans perhaps know best, that freedom is one of life's joys you can't put a price on.

Joanne Joseph
Johannesburg
February 2013

Acknowledgements

Vanessa Goosen

I had no idea of the physical, mental and spiritual strength I possessed until I experienced Lard Yao for sixteen years, six months and sixteen days. For this strength, which I needed in every aspect of my experience, I thank you, my saviour, Jesus Christ. I struggled to come to terms with being in prison for a crime I had no idea I was a part of, but in hindsight I thank you for this experience which humbled me and brought me closer to you.

You sent many angels to assist me in my journey and for all of their love and support, I thank you. To the first angels, Hilton, Melanie, Lerell and Tatum Holmes, you were unselfishly there from the beginning to support, believe in me and raise Felicia when she returned to South Africa. I will never be able to repay the love and support you gave me, but I thank you for every blessing, big and small, you gave and continue to give to Felicia and me. I never got the chance to personally thank you Melanie and this I still battle with, but I salute you my dear friend. You will never know the impact and strength I drew from your regular letters of encouragement and information of Felicia's progress. To the Holmes, Williams and Petersen families, thank you for accepting Felicia as one of your own and giving her your support and love.

To the angels who provided me with spiritual guidance on my

journey, Michael and Rachel McCarthy, Lourdes and Charles Holmes, Albert Blanc, Resa Sausa, Cheryl Yap Sausa, Susan Haney, Nora Nicholson and Eileen Boelkes, thank you. You have given your time and resources unselfishly to become angels laying spiritual foundations and being conduits of change in people's lives. Know that you have changed my life and that of many people.

Since my return from Thailand I have come to appreciate and value TIME. In this world where we undervalue time and are selfish to only spend it on the things that matters to us, I have come to realise the unselfish nature of the people who gave up their time to support and help me. You are truly angels that are changing this world for the better.

To Mpumelelo Nyoka, aka "Bond", you came from nowhere without any request to provide me with legal assistance and plead my situation back in South Africa and the world, thank you for your wisdom and support to me and my family. To my dear friend Paul Conell, you never gave up pleading my situation to the South African government and even when every door was shut, you continued pursuing options with the governments of South Africa and Thailand, as well as with local and international dignitaries. To you and your family I thank you for the time you invested in me. I received much support and love from so many angels from all over the world in the form of letters and visits. To all of you, who are too many to mention at this time, a huge thank you.

Special thanks to the people that wrote to and visited me regularly from South Africa. Elmarie Wessels, Norma Payne, Douglas Cohen, Chantel Larnyoh, Noel Andrews, Christelle Wells, Ivan Bjorkman, Kelly Hendricks, Dr Johan Strijdom, Marietha du Toit, Clara Joubert Maarshalk, Venitia Cohen and Chantal Joyce. You did not know me until you read about me in the media, yet you came to show me love. Your generosity and love for me and Felicia will always be appreciated and remembered.

To the friendships that were birthed from my experience in Thailand with Jeff Edhouser, Pauline Roeche, Phra Thitinyano, Nora Nicholson, Jack Slier, Matthew (Avero and family), Kay Danes, Notapol and Alida Srichomkwan and Per, to all of you a special thanks. You came from different parts of the world to support me. Every second you spent with me has helped me in my journey.

To all my family members who prayed for me and regularly wrote to me, thank you.

To Markus Gyssler, you are a special person who entered my life at a very difficult time while imprisoned. Thank you for your belief in me and your love for both Felicia and myself. To my lifelong friends Collette Holmes Afonso and Christine Gettly Osuagwu, your love and support to Felicia and me will always be treasured.

Being reintegrated was made easy by the support and love from my daughter Felicia. The thoughts of you being happy and loved back in South Africa brought me great comfort and eased the pain of longing to be with you. You are a beautiful soul with so much love inside of you and I am grateful for your support when I returned home. We cannot make up the lost time apart, but we can make the best of our time we are blessed with now.

To the people that assisted me with the challenging task of being reintegrated back into society, I humbly thank you. To Dr Marlin McKay, Reverend Carl Hendricks, Pastor Pretorius and Roger Kirkwood, know that I appreciate all your support.

Without the royal amnesties from the King of Thailand, I would still be serving time in Lard Yao. To you, King Bhumibol Adulyadej, thank you.

Then a very special thanks to the people who worked so hard with me to make this book happen. To the writers Joanne Joseph and Larissa Focke, thank you for sacrificing long hours and for your patience in bringing my story to the world.

I want to give a special thanks to my greatest critic and supporter, Rupert Henry, who stood by me and counselled me during my emotional break downs, who took me by the hand and carried me through this book.

To the inmates and staff of Lard Yao who became my family, I would like to thank you for assisting me to survive while there. Lard Yao become my home, as unbearable as it was with its concrete walls, prison bars and overcrowded rooms, but accepting my fate made my stay easier even when I did not know if I would ever see home again. A lesson learnt was that I had to work with what I had, and what I learnt was that I had TIME.

Thank you for your TIME to read and listen to my story. I pray that you will draw encouragement from my experience and better understand the value of your most precious possession: TIME. Invest it wisely and unselfishly as you will never know the impact it has on another person's life journey.

◯

Joanne Joseph

There are many people to whom I owe a huge debt of gratitude for playing a role, directly or indirectly, in the making of this book.

To Melinda, who believed wholeheartedly in the success of this project before I'd even put a word on the page and became a rigorous pre-dawn editor once I had – I hope some of your incredible writer's instinct will rub off; Bridget and the team at Jacana, thank you for your ongoing encouragement and support and treating this project with such love and care.

To my family: My amazing husband, Neil, thank you for being Mom and Dad, housekeeper, breadwinner and Masterchef while this book took shape. I can't imagine my life without you. To my precious Jade – this book is for you. In everything I do, you will always be my greatest inspiration to succeed. Reach high, above and beyond, my baby – you can do anything you dream of. To my outstanding parents, Andy and May, the "Chapter Police" who called me almost every day to check on my progress and never allowed me to give up! Where would I be without the investment of your time, your love, your belief since I was a child? And to my inspirational brother, Jeremy, who leads by example in his commitment to high standards – thank you, no matter where in the world you are, for always finding the time to read my work and share your astute thoughts with me.

Paulina French and Caitlin Todd, thank you for all your emotional and practical support while this book was being written.

You two are gold! Kenlynn Sutherland, perhaps this book is one of the culminations of the many seeds you planted as an exceptional teacher. I'll never forget what you've done for me. To the team at eNCA, especially Debora Patta – thank you for supporting me in this endeavour and in my work every day. A special thank you to all those who took time out of their busy schedules to endorse this book – I truly appreciate it. To all my friends and family who have buoyed me with your faith in me, your encouragement and your prayers, please be assured that every little bit has played a role in bringing this book together.

And finally, Vanessa – I know there were times when it wasn't easy, but thank you for sharing your story with me. I may not be able to give you sixteen and a half years back, but I can give you my words. I hope that in some way they will help you to move forward towards happiness.